WOMAN'S TRIUMPH

WOMAN'S TRIUMPH

ASHA RANAWAT

PUBLICATIONS

KALPAZ PUBLICATIONS

Delhi-110052

Woman's Triumph

Rs. 450

ISBN : 81 - 7835 - 508 - 6

Published in 2006 in India by
Kalpaz Publications,
C-30, Satyawati Nagar, Delhi-110052
E-mail : kalpaz@hotmail.com

Laser Type Setting by: Mega Graphics, Delhi
Printed at: Salasar Imaging System, Delhi

Dedication

I dedicate this humble offering to my Supreme Being, who inspired and compelled me to express my thoughts and life's experiences through this book.

My deep gratitude to the great Master of wisdom, Saints and Sages who taught me how to live a life in love and prefect harmony. And to use this precious human birth to attain the eternal bliss.

CONTENTS

List of Illustrations

Acknowledgement

I gratefully acknowledge the contribution of my family whose love has enriched my life. The upbringing that I received and the guidance of my parents helped me is shaping my life. I specially owe a lot to my highly spirited grand-mother who even at the age of 96 taught me the zest for life.

My Husband Dev and children Ronilla & Rohit have been my greatest strength and support.

Manish Sharma, Mrinal, Dr. Lovlin Thadani and some special friends helped me in time of need.

Amrit Dev Burman served me diligently while I was busy writing.

1
Introduction

Human psyche works in mysterious ways. Lately, as I entered the evening of my life, something strange began to happen. Every time, I closed my eyes to focus my attention on something or to meditate or pray, some pages from a book would appear before my eyes, with words written on them, which were so minute that howsoever hard I may try, I was unable to read them. This went on for a couple of years on end, but what these words conveyed remained an enigma for me.

Then one day during the early hours of the morning, when I was fast asleep, I heard a voice saying to me, "Write!" Suddenly I woke up and thought that most probably it might have been be a dream or a plain illusion. But when I turned over and slipped into a wakeful slumber, it happened again. This time the message was clear, 'Write a book based on your experiences'. I sat up on my bed thinking that I was no writer or a journalist then how could I do it? The next moment the answer came from somewhere within me that it was my inner voice that was asking me to do so. "If you have urged me to write, then you also have to show me the path to accomplish the task," I said.

Time passed, and somehow I forgot about the whole thing. About two months ago, once again those pages with minute words started appearing in front of my eyes. It was then that I decided to write this book.

It is well known that the *Ten Commandments*

appeared before *Moses*, which he passed on to the humanity. The only thing I would like to say humbly that most probably my inner voice wants me to share my life's experiences with you. I pray to my inner voice to bless me and guide me to find the right words and put me in touch with those people who would encourage me and help me accomplish this task. I am very optimistic about it because it is my inner voice, which has always guided me all through my journey in this world. I believe that it is the voice of the *Supreme Being*, of the Creator of this universe. An individual is only a minute part of this universe. To appreciate and to participate in this cosmic web of interdependence, you have to understand the one reality that pervades the universe. God, Nature or the Supreme Being is the one and only source of energy that keeps you going in this journey called life. Once this realization dawns on a person, the person begins to evolve spiritually, and then reaches a stage when he or she becomes complete in himself or herself. Complete in the sense that from thereon the person has to look only within to seek an answer to any problem that maybe troubling him or her. Such a person stops hankering after name, fame or worldly wealth and develops love and compassion for all forms of life. That does not mean that one rejects the boons of life that come one's way. One receives them humbly as the gifts of God and uses them in a way, which is not directed by one's ego, but by one's inner voice for the benefit of all. This inner voice or soul is the essence of an individual. It determines the behaviour of a person all through the thick and thin. It talks to the individual like a mentor guiding him or her at the right time. One often hears people saying, "My conscience or the inner voice did not allow me to do it!" It is this very conscience or inner voice that prevents a person from going astray and avoid the pitfalls of life. Unfortunately, people who lack this boon, bestowed upon an individual by God, follow the path dictated by their respective ego. Far from following the path of love and compassion for all forms of life, they exploit any opportunity that comes their way to fulfil their selfish desires. Since there is no end to these selfish desires, they end up getting more and more isolated from their fellow human beings. Such people are naturally cut off from the very source that sustains a person's life. They begin to treat other human beings, as well as the very environment in which they live, as simply a source of exploitation for their self-gratification. These are the people who perpetrate social crimes and get mired deeper and deeper into anti-social activities and lead wretched and lonely lives.

Life is a challenge. All of us have to face it as well as we can. Those who are blessed with an awakened conscience listen to their inner voice. They are the ones who are given opportunities to evolve spiritually and lead their lives in harmony with both nature and their fellow human beings. Every individual has to pass through a maze of temptations and struggle to get a hold on one's life and give it a direction, and reach a stage when one is at peace with oneself and the outer world. To reach this stage one needs tremendous endurance and patience. Having arrived one gains a certain poise and become fully aware of one's actions. Since every action has an equal and opposite reaction, such a person begins to scrutinize every action of his or her and also the thought process that leads to it. By doing so that person can navigate his conduct in such a way that every step is taken in the right direction.

One's ethos or the distinguishing character or the guiding beliefs evolve with growing awareness of the vast treasure of teachings which have been handed over to the humanity from time to time by the great souls like *Mahavir, Buddha, Moses, Christ, Mohammad* and *Nanak*. They showed various paths to humanity to lead happy, purposeful and peaceful lives in this world. The lives of these great souls have one thing in common. An uncompromising and relentless search for truth carried out with utmost honesty and sincerity. This very search lifts a person from the humdrum of daily life and puts one on the path of spiritual evolution. But in order to understand one's place in the universe, one must try and understand the creator and his creation.

The Creator and His Creation

The Universe with its boundless expanse in which countless galaxies, sun, stars and planets follow an orderly course, to say the least, is awe-inspiring. Our own planet - Earth - just a speck of this vast universe is unique. So far it is the only known planet where life flourishes. From a humble blade of grass to the creatures living in the water and outside including primates and human beings possessing instinctive/natural intelligence share this planet. Though life on earth has some common features, yet each one of God's creations is unique in itself. The same thing applies to human beings. Although they share many common traits, yet everyone is so different from the other.

Different regions on the earth are vastly different from each other. One country's geography is totally different from any other. So are the lives of the people. One has just to look at the faces of millions of people living in different parts of the globe to find that not only the colours of their skin, even the colour of their hair and eyes are different. Even more amazing is the fact that two persons living in the same region are so vastly different from each other. Even real brothers and sisters differ from each other in so many ways. Their characters, aims and aspirations are not the same. The obvious question is that what makes a person what he or she is? Who controls the destiny of an individual? Are we free to exercise our will? Or, are we just puppets going through motions of life according to a fixed plan pre-determined by a superior power? The scope of the individual will lies in choosing between confinement to the individual ego or submission to the cosmic Self (whatever name you choose to give it). Implied here is a choice, which gives an individual an opportunity to come out of the confines of one's ego and follow the path, which leads to his or her spiritual evolution. All of us are given this life to experience divinity, which lies dormant within all of us. The question is how to experience it? Most spiritually evolved people believe that despite all the intelligence and wisdom that a person may possess, such divine experience happens to one only with the grace of God. The only option open to a person is to strive towards evolution with absolute honesty and commitment. Very often a person experiences negative results. A person often realizes that everything he or she plans goes awry. Even in our day-to-day life things do not move in the expected direction. Things that a person wants to achieve never materialise, while things one never expected even remotely, happen. Under the circumstances, a person comes to the conclusion that there is something called destiny. Every individual treads the path decreed by destiny. Even the parents who give birth to their children cannot determine their future.

Invariably one observes that parents want to fulfil their own ambitions through their children. Every parent thinks that his or her child should be better than him or her. They keep goading the child to follow a more lucrative profession, go to a better college, university or a professional institution. Without gauging the natural aptitude of the child, they keep pushing him/her to do what they want, thus ending up making their children confused and unhappy. Their only objective in doing so is mostly to win the praise from people around. They want people to say, 'Look, what great parents they are! And how well their children are doing!' Most of the time when people meet, their talk revolves around their children. One often hears a parent saying, 'You know my son is going to be a lawyer.' Another one brags, 'When my daughter grows up, she is going to be a surgeon in a renowned hospital in the USA.' A third person says, 'My elder son, who is now studying in such and such school, is going to be hotelier, and the younger one, an architect.' But invariably things turn out to be altogether different. In life, during which a person hardly knows what is going to happen the next moment, it is immature to talk about things that are going to happen years later. Some of these parents who have committed the folly of taking complete charge of their children's future, watch with dismay, how their children's life has shaped up contrary to their expectations. Such a thing often has an adverse effect on the life of their children. Being under pressure to compete with other children, instead of cultivating friendship with the other children, they begin to envy and harbour feelings of hatred and jealousy for them, and that too at a young age. Wiser parents can easily curb this tendency in their children before it does any serious damage to their happy and healthy growth into adulthood.

Understanding parents let their children grow up in freedom and allow them to follow their natural aptitudes. Such children are invariably more successful in the careers they chose voluntarily and often lead comparatively happy and purposeful lives.

Let me give an example of my own son. He did his schooling from *Mayo College* (an old princely school) in *Ajmer* (*India*). It was a boarding school. After finishing his high school, he went to Saint *Stephens College in Delhi* (*India*). He did his masters and joined an old British Company, *J. Thomas* (*Tea tasting and auctioning company*) in *Calcutta.* He spent about three years in that company. One day he came and told me that he was not happy with the work he was doing. I asked him why is it so, son? He said that his soul does not find happiness in that kind of work. I was very unhappy to hear this from him and told him to carry on because it provided him a good opportunity to learn more about the trade. I can never forget his reply, which was, 'You taught us to find happiness wherever we can and my happiness doesn't lie here. I have taken almost two and half years to decide because I wanted to be very sure of myself. ' That was the end of our conversation. He took a complete 'U' turn and joined a fitness company. Today he is very happy that he found something where his soul was at peace with himself. He is doing extremely well for himdelf. He married a girl who is his soul mate. She is a graduate in International Law and is working for United Nations High Commission for Refugee(UNHCR) as a protection officer.

My daughter had finished her school and wanted to carry on studying to be a professional in some field. She got married at the age of 19, to a boy from an affluent family. It was an arranged marriage. But deep within herself, she kept looking for something that her heart yearned for and having found it, she did well in her life. Of course, at that point, little did she know that one day she would be an administrator cum coordinator of seventeen schools in *Karachi* & *Hyderabad*. She often wonders what made her choose teaching as a career, which actually turned out to be where her heart lay.

Lots of time we hang on to a job or business because others feel we must be great guys to be there. But if we were ever asked how we feel about it, the answer invariably would be that the grass is greener on the other side. How true? Often we let people run our lives and go on smothering our spirit day in and day out, or in other words we kill ourselves. One often hears people saying, "So and so did well in life, because in his/her case the situation was favourable. My situation isn't or wasn't. You don't know my life was full of difficulties." Don't let these negative thoughts rule your mind. Life is the greatest teacher. How we learn by it depends on every individual. A husband thinks his wife should change and vice versa. Children think parents must change according to their ways and vice versa. They go on wasting all their time, energy and life. Nothing changes, and one day life comes to an end. The best thing is not to wait for the circumstances, time, environment and people to change. One should try and change oneself because you can only change yourself and no one else. No one can impose one's thinking on others. People often blame and curse their luck and crib about their destiny, but the truth is that every great person too had to pass through the same situation, but came out of it by exerting his or her will power and inner strength which all of us possess. Once I read somewhere: *'If you face difficulty, first go around it to get out of it. If you cannot, try to go under it to come out of it, if you still cannot, try to go over it and if it is still insurmountable, then crush it, the victory will be all yours.* This is what great will power does. Only thing is that we hardly utilize this power, which resides within all of us as a great gift of the Master of the universe to us. The solution to this problem is to give space to promote healthy relationships amongst people who have been thrown together by fate. Keep in mind the following

One day everyone has to die. Therefore, there is no need to nurse grudges or try and take revenge. Nature takes care of it in its own way.

Don't worry about what others think about you, the important thing is, what you think of yourself.

Money has wings, fame is incidental, and character is the only thing, which always stays and sustains us.

RAT RACE: TODAY'S DOMINANT ABERRATION

I have observed that the youth all over the world is facing the problem of rat race and tried in my own humble way to find some solution for it. Wherever you look, you see people involved in a mindless rat race. We are working hard to outdo our colleagues. This race starts early in life when the child joins the school. All parents want their children to do extremely well; therefore, children have to work harder and harder to remain ahead of the others. Such children when outdistanced by others suffer psychologically. The same problem is further aggravated, when the parents goad their children to do better and achieve results, which are beyond their capability.

School/College education at the passing out stage requires doing one's best to secure best possible marks. Every year when results are declared one hears of suicides and attempted suicides. But that is not all. The worse thing is that a very large number of young people who are unable to secure high marks go around with heavy hearts, a sick mind, depressed, dejected, but no one pays any attention to them.

After college, everyone finds a slot somewhere, either by going for higher education or finding a job. Anyway, whatever they choose to do, rat race ensues. After one starts working, one wants to outperform one's colleagues. Earlier, it was the parents who were after the child, now it is your own life partner who keeps reminding you to work harder and do better. You still remain stuck in the rat race; making your own life miserable, facing constant tension, rejoicing only in your own success and the downfall of your competitors.

I have so far dwelled on the vast majority of people who are running this mindless rat race. However, there is a small percentage of people who chose not to take part in this rat race. Such people are either too dumb or far too intelligent to get involved in a thing like that.

Their lives started by not being pushed around by their elders. They were generally those children who knew and understood what was good for them. They refused to burden themselves with unnecessary work. They were intelligent enough to apply their minds to the areas of their interest. In later life, they chose specialisation that others had not even ventured upon and became pioneers in their respective fields with little or no competition. Thus they chalked out their own paths without entering the rat race.

Parents must realize when and how much to push their children. They must assess both the strong and the weak side of their children. Children must be helped to cash in on their strong points and rectify their weaknesses. A child should not be given a feeling that he has to run a race from the very beginning. What is important is that he should have a satisfactory career and a happy and healthy future. This is easier said then done. But, then one has to rely on one's common sense and intelligence.

If you pick up the biographies of people who have done well in life, you will find that about 60 percent of them were mediocre students in school/college, but when they entered field of their choice, they turned out to be either pioneers or people who took on with courage in life based on their intelligence and practical common sense. Most of them were strong willed, honest to the core and God-fearing. Keeping in view the students community in particular, *Abraham Lincoln's* advice is excellent. His famous letter to the Principal of his son's school speaks volumes about this problem:

"He will have to learn, know, that all men are not just, all men are not true. But teach him also that for every scoundrel there is a hero, that for every selfish politician, there is a dedicated leader. Steer him away from envy, if you can. Teach him the secret of quiet laughter. Let him learn early that bullies are the easiest to lick... Teach him, if you can, the wonder books... but also give him quiet time to ponder over the eternal mystery of birds in the sky, bees in the sun, and flowers on a green hillside."

"In school, teach him that it is far more honourable to fail than to cheat...Teach him to have faith in his own ideas, even if everyone tells him they are wrong...Teach him to be gentle with gentle people, and tough with the tough. Try to give my son the strength not to follow the crowd when everyone is getting on the bandwagon. Teach him to listen to all men, but teach him also to filter all he has heard on the screen of truth, and take on the good that comes through it."

"Teach him, if you can, how to laugh when he is sad... teach him that there is no shame in tears. Teach him to scoff at cynics and to beware of too much sweetness...Teach him to sell his brawn and brain to the highest bidders, but never to put a tag on his heart and soul. Teach him to close his ears to the howling mob...and to stand and fight if he thinks he's right.

"Teach him gently, but do not cuddle him, because only the test of fire makes fine steel. Let him have the courage to be impatient...Let him have the patience to be brave. Teach him always to have sublime faith in himself, because then he will always have sublime faith in mankind."

In our current situation when we are running that rat race, undergoing all that stress and strain, we overlook one major factor. That is the existence of that super power which controls the destiny of an individual. Without going into the intricacies involved in this belief, it is enough to say that there is a power, whatever you call it, which holds the universe together. We are his creation. He is the only source of energy, which keeps us going. When that energy is withdrawn, we die. Faith in God is a great energy giver and stress remover.

Yoga, an ancient Indian attainment – a system of exercises for attaining bodily and mental control and well-being, preaches that the soul (*Atma)* can discover the God (*Parmatma)* through meditation and practising various *Kriyas* involved in meditation i.e. travelling within. The scriptures describe the realisation of God as a state of ever-lasting bliss.

Most of us need meditation even if it be for 20 minutes a day. We should introduce meditation in our education system. How easy it is for children to successfully meditate has only to be seen to be believed. It takes away a lot of stress from the children – mothers, would do well to make it a point to help children meditate before going to sleep at night

Meditation can help a child cope with his studies. Moreover, this is one certain way for the elders to find the divine within themselves. It also helps a person in the following manner:

(i) It improves one's power of concentration.

(ii) It strengthens the character of an individual.

(iii) It makes a person more relaxed and ward off stress, if any

(iv) It strengthens a person's faith in God.

Father

Mother

Grand Mother

Dev and I at a family wedding
July (2005)

Father-in-law Shri Bhawani Singh Ranawat of Kakerwa at young age.

With grandsons Shiv Karan, Francesco and Bhawani at Rohit's house in Kathmandu, Nepal June (2003).

Our Jaipur House.

Myself, Dr. Pritipal Singh, Giulia, Rohit, Dev and Ronilla. Shiv Karan Singh standing in front of his father at Rohit's Wedding Dec. (1998).

Brothers - L.R.- Hari Singh, Sangram Singh, Narendra Singh
Standing- L.R.- Ajay Singh, Myself and Vijay Singh.
Golden Wedding Anniversary
Function of Uncle Raj and Aunt Rama.

(Two inseparable brothers) Father and Uncle Raj
Francesco in between the two at farm house.

Amitabh Bachchan, me and Rajamata Gayatri Devi at a function (13.11.2001).

Chief of Army Staff General N.C. Vij, Mrs. Rita Vij and myself at an Army Function.

L.R. Ronilla, Karan, Bhawani, I and Giulia in Stein Am Rhine in Europe (2002).

Hildegard, Dev and I, at De Plasmolen in Boxmeer (Holland).

Collection of wall plates (souvenirs) collected from different countries.

With friend Traute in Germany summer (2000).

2
My Life

I was born in *Jaipur* cantonment on 16 April, 1948, where my parents *Capt. Raghubir Singh* and *Mrs. Kailash Rathore* then lived. I was the only girl in a family of five. My elder brother Sangram Singh was fifteen months older to me and my younger brother, Narendra Singh, was exactly fifteen months younger. I started my education in Jaipur in 1953 and continued to study in various schools in *Nasiradab, Jammu* and *Poona.* In 1957 my father, then a Major, got posted to *Egypt* on a *UNO* assignment. On his return to India in 1960, he was posted to National Defence Academy in Kharagwasla near Poona as an instructor. This was one of the most enjoyable period of my early life. It was there that I learned to play a lot of outdoor games. Swimming became a passion with me. In early teens, I also learnt Bharat Natyam and English Ball Room dancing but could not pursue dance later because of Dev, my husband, who did not like dancing. Slowly the desire to dance died within me. I studied in Poona commuting everyday from my home to school. My brothers studied mostly in boarding schools. In my school in Poona, I learnt French as my second language but could not make any use of it till I visited *Switzerland* in my later life. *Geneva* is a French-speaking city and I enjoyed talking to people in my broken French. It's a very soft and sweet language. It is said that nothing learnt ever goes a waste. How true it turned out to be!

We came back to **Jaipur** in 1963 where I joined MGD Public School. I passed out of high school in

1965 and also learnt Rajasthani folk dances, which I continued to perform at our family weddings. Soon afterwards I got married to then *Lieut. R.V.S. Ranawat* (*The Guards*) on 22 June 1965. It was an arranged marriage. I was a young girl of seventeen. Being the only daughter in the *Rajawat Clan* of village Sodha, I was a pampered child, a bit of a Tom boy, knowing little in terms of running a house hold, because of which I did face a certain amount of difficulty in the first six months of our married life. Dev and my father fought in the Indo-Pak war during this period. It was then that I resolved and learnt everything possible to make myself an efficient housewife and in due course to be a great mother of two (a girl and a boy). At a very young age, I realized that life was very short and taught myself to live it on my own terms and not according to other people's dictates. It dawned upon me that in trying to please others endlessly, I would not and could not be true to myself. And the ability to be true to oneself is the most valuable gift that anyone's life has to offer.

Ronilla, the elder one of my two children was born to us at *Udaipur* on 18th February 1967. Dev, then a Captain got posted to *Shillong* (*Meghalaya*), an excellent hill station. While in Shillong, I was able to do a lot of horse riding. There were beautiful hills and valleys all around.

Shillong has a most beautiful natural golf course where Dev played a lot of golf. We travelled with our little daughter and saw the whole of *Nagaland, Mizoram, Assam, Sikkim, NEFA* and *West Bengal*. There were many tea gardens in Assam where some of my uncles and relations were working as tea planters. We enjoyed their hospitality, especially that of my father's younger cousin brother *Bahadur Singh* and my aunt *Asha*. Back in *Shillong* my daughter too started mounting a horse and she went everywhere with her *saise* holding on to the reins of her horse.

Our stay in *Shillong* was very enjoyable. At the time *Mr. B.K. Nehru* was the Governor of *Assam* and *Meghalaya.* His Hungarian wife arranged wonderful coffee parties inviting officers' wives and taught us how to bake Hungarian cakes and some other goodies. She was a very talented housewife. Shillong Club too organised lots of parties where all the participants had a lot of fun. Every Sunday morning we played Tambola. A very talented lady named *Mrs. Zaheer*, also took classes in her house and taught us Ikebana, the Japanese art of flower-arrangement that emphasizes form and teaches balance in accordance with strict rules.

Having served in *Shillong* for a couple of years, Dev was posted to a non-family station in 1969; I shifted to my parents place in Delhi along with my daughter, where my father was then posted. I was still living with my parents when my son Rohit was born on 25th October 1970. Both my infant son and daughter, who was 3 years and 8 months old at that time, were lucky to grow in an atmosphere of immense love and affection showered on them by their grandparents. *Rohit* was also lucky to have *Kanta* as his Nanny. A live-in maid, who took care of him almost like a mother. In 1971, my husband again went to the front to fight a war. This was his second war in six years, the first being in 1965 soon after our marriage.

After a year Dev was posted to *Meerut (U.P.).* Being a Remount and Veterinary Corps Centre, we had the best of horses. This gave me an opportunity to resume horse-riding seriously so as to excel. It was during this very period that I visited various places in northern India taking part in many competitions. During my absence *Kanta* mothered Rohit and took good care of Ronilla. I reached my zenith in horse riding carrier in 1973, when I won some coveted prizes at the national level organized at the Red Fort, Delhi.

In December 1973, Dev then a Major was posted to Poona. I loved being in Poona as I had spent a part of my childhood here and had studied at St. Mary's School here. Now that I was here with my children I made good use of my previous stay over there.

Ronilla too joined *St. Mary's* and a year later Rohit joined St. Bishop's. As a child Rohit, was a bit of an introvert but very affectionate.

Ronilla on the other hand was full of life. Between the two of them Ronilla was a great support to me. Being an outgoing child, she always had everyone's support as she had the knack of making everyone happy by going out of the way to please anyone she met. Rohit was a simple but a loving boy who rarely troubled anyone. Both the children were very close to their father who always sided with them when they played pranks on their mother.

But soon *Dev* had to move out of *Poona* on a posting to *Sikkim* in May 1976. The children and I continued to stay in Poona till October 1978. During this period, I kept myself usefully occupied and acquired Diploma in Interior Decoration in which I stood second in Maharashtra, did a course in Nursery Teacher's Training, as well as in Advance Ikebana and making crape paper flowers. I also held an exhibition of Ikebana flower arrangement at R.S.I. Club in Poona on 22nd December 1974. There were 75 exhibits, which were greatly appreciated by discerning local gentry. That was not all. Along with all that I also qualified as a beautician. I learned shorthand and typing. Later on I was able to make good use of what I had learnt when in the year 1999 I did interior designing of a hotel known as *'Kailrugji'*, which was owned by my younger brother. It gave me a wonderful opportunity to design and furnish many rooms and common areas like lounges and passages. I was thus able to pass those two years gainfully at Poona during the absence of Dev.

By the middle of 1978, children and I came to *Udhampur* (*J&K*) to join my husband who was posted there as a part of battalion. In *Udhampur* we spent one year and experienced the typical battalion life. There every family lived like a part of the extended family. Though families lived in separate houses but every now and then there were get-togethers, in which everyone was treated like a member of a large family. Thereafter, in June 1979, Dev was posted to *Ferozepur*. There I spent my time partly teaching in an army school also partly putting to use my beautician's training and running Yoga and Ikebana classes. Doing all these things along with managing my well-organised house gave me immense confidence and mental satisfaction.

In 1980 Dev was promoted and moved to command 11 Guards (Brigade of the Guards) *Batallion* as a *Colonel* in *Sikkim*. I decided to move to *Jaipur* and spend some time with my parents at the *Rajawat* farm where they now lived. By this time my father had retired. Six months before leaving *Ferozepur*, the children were put into the boarding schools. Ronilla joined *Maharani Gayatri Devi Girls Public School* and Rohit joined the *Mayo College* at Ajmer. While living with my parents I had almost nothing to do except to look after the garden at the *Rajawat* farms. I felt strangely uncomfortable. Since I had always been a very hard working person, this forced leisure was telling on my psyche.

It was then that I decided to make a trip to Europe. I had always been very fond of travelling and seeing new places. So I immediately got busy in putting plans into practice. For this venture, I was partly funded by Dev and partly by my younger brother. At the end of my tour to Europe I decided to stay in *London* (*U.K.*) where I had already made arrangement to pursue an advanced course in beauty and hair dressing. Luckily Dev's cousin sister was already living in *London.* She welcomed me with open arms. During my stay, besides doing the course, I saw every place worth seeing in London. While in *London*, I shopped for my *beauty salon*, which I wanted to set up once back in India, and also did some very selective shopping from *Harrods*, the world famous store, for our household and family. My trip to Europe did wonders in expanding my horizon and giving me a discerning vision. I was reasonably independent and confident before but this trip further enhanced these traits in my personality.

I returned from London on 30th June 1981. It was a sheer coincidence that the person who had the contract of *Rambagh Palace Hotel Beauty Salon* expired. The management was looking around for someone competent to take care of the same. I had all the qualifications required for the job. I applied and got the contract to run the beauty salon in 1981. This was my chance to be something on my own. I did a wonderful job. My skills as a beautician won a widespread recognition. Since then I carried on doing this job for well over two decades. During this period both my children got married, settled down and while Dev retired from the army in August 1995, I gave up my business in March 2003.

During these years I travelled extensively. I visited *South East Asia* thrice, went to *Burma* and *Japan* once, *USA* thrice. I went to *Europe* four times with Dev and stayed for almost a year in *Geneva* (*Switzerland*) with my family. Actually both my children were posted in Europe and *USA*, which gave me the opportunity to go and stay with them. Even today I love to meet people from different places and make new friends. I made four memorable visits to Pakistan, once with Dev.

MY WORKING LIFE

For a year, I taught in a K.G. School as a part-time teacher from 1978 to 1979, but later on, being a qualified beautician, set up my own business. It gave a new dimension to my personality. I was exposed to a different world. People from all parts of the world came to my salon and I loved interacting with them. While doing so, I realized human- beings everywhere have so much in common. Everyone likes simple, honest and straightforward people. Once you exchange notes, you shed so many wrong notions and come closer to each other. It was during this time of my life that I learnt a lot about life itself. One can never understand life in all its dimensions until one interacts with all sorts of people. At times, my relations with people had a troublesome beginning but ended on a harmonious note. It takes all sorts of people to make this world and to understand them you need a lot of patience, perseverance and positiveness.

One often comes across very nice and humane people. They have no complexes and are generally very amiable. They spread happiness wherever they go. But you also come across people who are full of complexes. There is nothing straight about them. They only know how to inflict pain and cause bitterness wherever they go. These types of people at best can be termed as sadists. It gives them great pleasure to make others suffer. I found many such people in every walk of life. It took me a lot of time to reconcile to the idea that such people are, by their very nature, petty, shallow, mean, jealous and unreasonable, the qualities that are believed to be so rampant in women. But the thing that I found most difficult to digest was that such men invariably treat women in a shabby manner. Having lived in the company of army officers since my childhood, I took it for granted that all men are gentleman and treat women like ladies. They not only stand up but spring up to pay their respect to a lady as soon as she steps into a party, public place, office or home. Being pampered, the only way of life I knew, certainly spoilt me! I used to be aghast whenever I witnessed a thing like that. I must say that I was lucky, in the sense that my clients never ever created a problem for me. They all respected me and in return I respected them.

There is a little incident, which rankled my mind for quite sometime. There was a gentleman, who being in authority thought no end of himself and perhaps was never taught how to behave with a lady. For petty things he harassed ladies. So much so that he didn't even spare his own wife. One day he ordered his own wife to clean the cobwebs on the ceiling due to which she had a terrible accident and nearly lost her legs. She climbed up a wooden cupboard with the help of a stool. The cupboard had a glass top. As she put her weight on its edges, which had wooden planks, she lost the balance and slipped on the glass top, which broke under her weight. Both her legs scraped through the broken glass cutting all her veins. The damage was so severe that she could barely walk for a number of years. Perhaps her husband was not aware of it but I was convinced that this was the punishment he received because of his own actions.

People with low self-esteem usually avoid meeting bright, intelligent and confident people. They prefer the company of inferior people who are not well educated and come from lower social strata of the society. You too must have come across such people. They look bored and dejected. Such people are lethargic and completely unconscious of their personal failings. They have no desire to improve their lives. Their greatest failing is their refusal to come out of their self-created shells and interact with others. Their interaction even with their own families i.e. wives and children is marginal. Such people lead a miserable life and are a source of spreading misery in the society.

Having said so much about some undesirable characters that one often come across in life, I would introduce some really admirable people I have come across in my life, who not only set an example for their fellow human beings for leading noble lives and inspiring others to do so but also spreading happiness and sunshine wherever they go. Apart from shouldering their personal responsibilities, they also dedicate their lives for the welfare of the people around them.

While going through one's life, one comes across innumerable people. People come together in educational institutions, work places, or even when they are going on a journey in a train or an aeroplane. But the mysterious thing about life is that among those thousands of people that one meets, most are forgotten completely, a large number remain mere acquaintances whom one rarely recalls or meets again, but some people do come close to each other. Even among such people there are many who soon drift away. But then, the most fascinating thing is that a few of them do enter into a meaningful relationship becoming life long friends.

How it happens is a mystery. It is something which will require serious research to unravel it. My only purpose is to introduce some people whom I met, learned to admire and grew closer to them for one reason or the other.

The first person that immediately comes to my mind is *Her Highness Rajmata Gayatri Devi of Jaipur.* She is a living legend. Formerly, princess of *Cooch Behar* she married His Highness *Mansingh* of Jaipur and made quite an impact on the people of Jaipur by her valuable contribution to the Jaipur state. She was the one who opened renowned schools in Jaipur, known as Maharani Gayatri Devi Girls Public School and *Swai Mansingh* Public School in which she introduced co-education. She established *Chand Shilpshala* in Jaipur, an institute for women, which provided different courses for the women who wanted to take up a career for themselves. I happened to be the member of this Institute. This institute gave the best possible training to its students in a wide range of subjects like tailoring, painting, music, dancing, a beautician's course in beauty upkeep or learning the art of tie and dye along with making people proficient in using computers. She also opened two schools in two villages. One in *Jagon Ki Bowary* and the other in *Isharda*, which gave, free education to poor children.

Rajmata Gayatri Devi is a remarkable person. She was not only amongst the ten most beautiful women of the world in 40's but also made history in Rajasthan by remaining a member of the Indian Parliament for 17 long years at a stretch and also entering her name in Guinness Book of World Records by winning a seat by the highest number of votes cast by the people of her constituency in her favour. She is undoubtedly a lady of substance, intelligence, possessing admirable qualities of both head and heart.

Maharaja Sawai Jai Singh Benevolent Trust is a trust run by Rajmata as a charitable organisation to help the poor, disabled, widows and other needy people to alleviate their sufferings as best as it can.

Rajmata Gayatri Devi knew our family, but she came to know me personally or more intimately after I took over the beautician's establishment in Rambagh Palace which is owned by the Royal family. She liked me as a person and often invited me to some extraordinary parties she threw at the Lilly Pool Palace where I had the chance to meet many celebrities from all over the world. Festivals like Diwali, Dashera, Shard Purnima, Shankrant and birthday parties were a regular feature every year. I can never forget the care and concern she showed for me all through, and especially when Dev was away. Once I was so touched when Her Highness brought *Jacqlene Onasis* and her son *John F. Kennedy* (Jr.) to meet me at Rambagh Palace. Unfortunately today both the mother and son are no more.

They say that life is made up of coincidences and their absence. It so happened that on 16th April, 1997 Her Highness sent me a letter asking me to be a trustee for *Maharaja Sawai Jai Singh Benevolent Trust.* I was its trustee for one year and later its honorary secretary. I looked after the trust for seven years from 1997-2004. These seven years I worked for the trust with all my heart and soul and saw to it that my accountant kept an account of every penny and ensured that the money went to the right person. In a way this association has been very satisfying for me in the sense that it gave me a chance to learn from an extraordinary person like Rajmata Gayatri Devi. When I resigned from my business after 22 years in 2003, I also resigned from the trust a year later to regain my 'freedom' in every sense of the word.

Another pretty, charming and a very confident person who became a very good friend of mine is *Princess Rajshree of Bikaner.* Being a sports oriented person and having won some coveted prizes in horse-riding, I was first attracted to her when she was awarded *'Arjuna Award'*, the highest national award for sports in 1968 when she emerged as number one shooter (Rifle) in India.

I again had a chance to be with her in *London* when Rajmata invited both *Rajshree* and her family and myself for dinner at her *Sloan Square* Residence.

Later when I met Princess Rajshree in Rambagh Palace in Jaipur, thereafter I had many opportunities to meet her every now and then and found her to be a very amiable and affectionate person who responded with exceptional warmth. Rajshree and myself became very good friends. It was through the courtesy extended by her that I saw the length and breadth of Bikaner in style.

It is a privilege to have a caring friend like Rajshree. Among other things I really admire the way she has taken all her late father's responsibilities! Late His Highness Karani Singh brought her up like a son. Today when her father is no more, she has shown to the world to be his worthy successor by looking after the people of *Bikaner.* It is she who takes care of all their palaces and properties in India and *U.K.* Apart from running a historical museum, which has some rare exhibits, she is running a charitable trust for the people of Bikaner, which provides medical and financial aid to those in distress.

Another person who became a friend of mine is *Rooplata Kumari.* I have known her since I was a student of Maharani Gayatri Devi Girls Public School. She was my senior by many years and was considered a great beauty. Senior girls were addressed as *jijas* in our school and I too called her Jija (elder sister). It is difficult to come across a more talented person. There is hardly anything that she can't do. She is an exporter and made a name for herself by making exclusive carpets and designing a mini palace for herself, which has won praise from experts for her discerning taste, beauty and class. Her husband *Harinder Pal Singh* and she have also designed a Resort, which is cited as an extraordinary example of their skills in interior designing and decoration. Her sense of dressing up, soft voice and the warmth she exudes can win anybody's heart. Among her other talents is the choice of food served at her parties, which people remember for days together. She arranges everything to perfection. Mr. Harinder Pal Singh, known as Henry to his friends have always delighted me with a special talent of his. Whatever colour of *saree* I wear for their party, he has the knack of mixing and matching the same coloured cocktail or mocktail for me. I call him jijosa (sister's husband). I am very fond of the couple and love to be with them at their mini palace and resort. They are blessed with two handsome sons, *Inderjeet* and *Udayjeet*. The whole family works as a team in perfect harmony.

Another remarkable person is *Dr. A. Rahman* whom I met in Delhi through a common friend, *Mrs. Mumtaz Baqar*. Dr. Rahman taught me not only the fundamentals of Muslim faith but also much about Sufism, which along with Bhakti Movement laid the foundation of a composite Indian culture. Dr. Rahman was one of those rare people who despite being an eminent scientist was an ocean of knowledge on Sufism and a true sufi himself. Right from the beginning of our association I always treated him like my brother and always addressed him as *bhai* (brother). He has written some significant books on subjects like History of Science, Science and Society and Development Studies. He retired as the Founder Director of The National Institute of Science, Technology and Development Studies, Delhi. He has taught me a great deal about Sufism. While talking to him one finds him amazingly well informed. I am close to bhai and his wife *Shaffo*, whom I call *aapa*, who herself is a well-read person and a true soul-mate to her husband.

Apart from these people, we being very much a part of the Indian army, my husband Dev and I developed some long-lasting friendships within the army circles. Before I introduce some of our friends from the army, I would like to share with you some of my observations regarding our friendships, which have lasted decades and are still going strong. Besides comradeship which the army personnel share, I found most of them to be straightforward, honest, upright and dignified people who cared for the feelings of people they came in contact with and always showed sensitive concern for the suffering of others. I am not sure but I have a feeling that this must be because of what they went through while fighting battles to defend the honour of their beloved country and its people.

Amongst others *General N.C. Vij*, who later became Chief of Army Staff and his lovely wife *Rita* have been our very good friends for a very long time. One great quality of Rita and Nirmal Vij that has always impressed Dev and me is their stark simplicity and humbleness. Even as the Army Chief, living under tight security, the couple would accompany me to the door of my car whenever I went to see them. During our long service in the army, both the families kept in touch with each other and never missed a chance to be together. One thing that I would like to share is that Rita, who is a very simple person by nature, happens to be a wonderful cook. Despite having help, she always makes it a point to cook for her friends. Having food made by her has always been a treat and something that one always looks forward to with great eagerness.

Indira Kumar, wife of General *A.R. Kumar* and I grew up as young wives of army officers and became very good friends. It is almost three decades since our families have maintained live contact with each other. Wherever they were, they never forgot to communicate with us and enquire into the welfare of our family. Come what may, the two families never fail to exchange New Year's greetings. It has been going on for years and hopefully will go on in the future. There is a mutual desire to meet each other. Recently I joined them on the happy occasion of their daughter's wedding. We may meet after a gap but whenever that happens, we feel as if we have always been together.

Urvashi, wife of *Brigadier Surjit Singh*, is a true and reliable friend of mine. You call her up in the middle of the night and she is sure to be by your side in the morning. She has an obsession to help people. Once she comes to know someone is in distress, she goes out of her way to be of help. She is a sensitive soul who gets tormented on seeing so much pain and misery in this world. She feels so distraught on seeing a miserable beggar on the roadside that I often tease her by saying, 'Why don't you invite him for a cup of coffee or a meal?' And she laughs, the bubbly laughter of an innocent child. Once I received a call from someone in Delhi asking me if he could meet Urvashi on my next visit to Delhi. He told me there was a special reason for his wanting to meet her. After a month, I went to meet the gentleman concerned along with Urvashi. The reason why he wanted to meet Urvashi was to find out as to what kind of hold I had on my friend that the latter was ready to run around for some work I had assigned to her in the scorching heat of the afternoon sun! He told us that he had never seen such a true friend before. We both laughed and he understood that we were actually jolly good friends. It was then that I made it very clear to him that my friends were my greatest treasure and that I nurture the friendship with my sincere friends that are hard to come by in today's world.

Indian Army Officer's Wife

The best time of my life being married to an Army officer was when Dev was commanding *11th Guard Batallion* in *Ranchi* after coming from *Yakhla Pass.* The love and affection from our brother officers and wives and of course not forgetting the men

(*Jawans*) and their families are to stay in our hearts - a true family in every way. Being busy with my work at Jaipur, it was always a *flying* visit to Ranchi. Finally, when we had to say goodbye after Dev's posting orders, we all cried like small children.

Here I would like to point out some peculiar problems of being an army officer's wife, especially being the wife of an Infantry Officer. Their husbands being away from home on postings to non-family stations or field areas on borders, for more than a half of their service years, the entire responsibility of looking after themselves and their families falls on their shoulders.

Under the circumstances, an army officer's wife has to take all sorts of decisions, regarding running of her home, children's education and so on independently. Because of that she not only becomes a man of the house in the absence of her husband but also has to behave like one. By and large the Indian society and especially the men still think that a single lady is a frail creature and would need a man around to run a home and to take care of children. Mostly the attitude of male members of the society is such that they do not pay proper attention to a lady's problem or complaint. Even in schools and colleges, the principals always expect the mother and father to come together to know about their child's progress. Since an army officer's wife has to handle everything herself, she becomes strong, independent and self-reliant. In the process she becomes so confident that she can manage almost everything on her own. She learns to handle all the out-door work like taxes, insurance, renewal of licenses with great efficiency. In case the couple decides to build their own house, in the absence of her husband, then dealing with architects, engineers, contractors and labourers also becomes a part of her work.

An army officer's wife is invariably a good and competent mother to her children. One can see for oneself how defence services officers' children make a success in whatever field they choose to enter. Some of the beauty contestants to Miss Universe and Miss World also come from army, air force and navy background. The credit goes to their mothers for inculcating a great deal of confidence in their off springs.

By and large, the children with army background are educated, talented, smart and creative. Their manners are impeccable because of which they gain respect wherever they go. Confidence and maturity make them stand out in any crowd. What all have they gone through to become what they are, no one can ever imagine! How upright, dignified they are! The children of an army officer's wife are her biggest reward. Her children alone know what their mother has gone through! Army officers' wives are true Indian wives who strain every nerve for the welfare of their family. Men can seldom appreciate their silent contribution in raising children... Few can sacrifice as much as these women can. Even their husbands have to depend on them after retirement because of their lack of experience in dealing with the civilians. The men often feel insulted when someone does not respond to them with respect that they are used to in the army. People must realize that the wives of the army personnel too need to be pampered or at least given a pat on their back fighting a lonesome battle of running their homes single-handedly. But surprisingly, their husbands coolly forget the sacrifices made by their wives after their retirement.

The kind of responsibility army officers' wives shoulder is phenomenal. At times, they walk like a man, talk like a man (loud) and behave like a man, but deep down they remain true women, in every way. I salute these women!

Once my niece *Chavvi* sent me a nice e-mail which impressed me so much that I am quoting verbatim:

"A little boy asked his mother, "Why are you crying?" "Because I'm a woman," she told him.

"I don't understand", he said. His mom just hugged him and said, "And you never will."

Later the little boy asked his father, "Why does mother seem to cry for no reason?"

"All women cry for no reason", was all his dad could say.

The little boy grew up and become a man, still wondering why women cry. Finally he put in a call to God. When God got on the call, the boy asked, "God why do women cry so easily?"

God said, "When I made the woman she had to be special."

"I made her shoulders strong enough to carry the weight of the world, yet gentle enough to give comfort."

"I gave her inner strength to endure child birth and the rejection that many times comes from her people."

"I gave her a hardness that allows her to keep going when everyone else gives up, and take care of her family through sickness and fatigue without complaining."

"I gave her the sensitivity to love her children under any and all circumstances, even when her child has hurt her very badly."

"I gave her strength to carry her husband through his *faults* and fashioned her from his rib to protect his heart."

"I gave her wisdom to know that a good husband never hurts his wife, but sometimes tests her strengths and her resolve to stand beside him unfalteringly. And finally, I gave her a tear to shed. This is hers, exclusively to use whenever it is needed."

"You see my son," said God, "the beauty of a woman is not in the clothes she wears, the figure that she carries, or the way she combs her hair. The beauty of a woman must be seen in her eyes, because that is the doorway to her heart – the place where love resides."

My Family

My late *grand parents* from my father's side especially my *grand mother* really knew the art of living. I still remember, when we were with her, we never experienced a dull moment. She lived till the ripe age of 96. She was totally dedicated to her family. My grand mother told us that the secret of her happy life is: Love for all. She often expressed her philosophy in these words, "You are free when you love, and enslaved when you hate. Pride destroys you, but your humility wins over others. Be humble, keep your house in order and for the rest do not worry about anything." She was a God-fearing person and had a very good rapport with her God. She often told us that whenever she prays to God for something, He listens to her. She loved and blessed her progeny all the time. My grandfather Thakur Pratap Singh, on the other hand, was a very strict and disciplined man. The whole family respected him and looked up to him with awe. He was an aristocrat and lived like one all through his life.

My *grandmother* and *grandfather*, when satisfied that they had discharged all their responsibilities towards their family in particular and the society at large, in their ripe old age went on a pilgrimage to *Dwarka, Badrinath, Rameshwaram* and *Puri* known as four *Dhams* (considered the most sacred religious places of Hindus). Many Hindus look forward to performing this ritual after retiring from social responsibilities. After their *Teerathyatra* or pilgrimage, the *Ganges* water that they brought home with themselves had to be distributed. Consequently, a big function was organised in our village known as *Gangoj*, where not only the whole village but also people from the adjoining villages, were invited to a feast. It was more elaborate than a wedding function. We ourselves witnessed it as small children. First a big *Hawan* (oblation to fire goddess) took place in which many Pundits recited *mantras* in unison during the ceremony. For me it was more like a fun-fare.

My *grand mother* whose name was *Sajjan Kanwar*, who hailed from the *Royal* family of *Kishengarh*, was a great story-teller and, at night, before going to bed, she lulled us to sleep with one of her fascinating stories. All her grand children loved her. She had two sons, my father being the older one. She always said, "They are my *Ram* and *Laxman*". Those words uttered by my grandmother remain true even after the passage of so many years. Both the brothers love and are truly devoted to each other. Their relationship can be cited as an example in our society even today. My uncle is 82 and my father is in the

84th year of his life.

My father *Raghubir Singh*, retired from the Indian army as a *Brigadier* having won *Mahavir Chakra*, the highest gallantry award in 1965 war. He retired from the army in the year 1975. My uncle, *Raj Singh*, retired as *Deputy Inspector General* from Police in 1982, and he too was awarded Police Medal for his meritorious services. My grand mother told us that one of her wishes was that both her sons flew flags on their cars. Like many of her other wishes, this one too had come true. All her grand children, that is two of my brothers, *Major Sangram Singh* and *Narendra Singh*, three of my other brothers, i.e., my uncle's sons, *Hari Singh*, *Vijay Singh* and *Lt. Colonel Ajay Singh* grew up as a part of a very close and well-knit family. I have always treated my uncle's sons as my real brothers, as the word cousin was alien in our homes. We all belonged to one family. Even when my uncle and father were posted in different places while they were in service, all of us always got together at least once a year for two months during our summer vacations at my father's house. My brother Hari grew up with us as he had always lived with us ever since his early childhood. My brothers went to boarding schools but Hari always stayed with us. Imagine my plight being their only sister. At times all of them ganged up and teased me driving me to tears. But being boys' company, I too became a bit of a tomboy. Like them, I also became fairly tough and independent. Vijay and Ajay were much younger. So I stood an even chance to deal with them, but Narendra and Hari were very mischievous. I was rather scared of them but being older they saw to it that they didn't hurt me. Together we had a wonderful time and I loved them all.

My Father has always been a role model to

me. Honest and truthful to the core, he is an upright, dignified and a straightforward person. He is fiercely independent, takes his own decisions, rather than playing second fiddle to anyone. He leads an exemplary life based on the time-tested values so dear to the *Rajputs*. With God's grace he is fortunate, in the sense that being the scion of a notable family, he has always been well-off financially. He is a handsome man, with pleasing manners. His aura exudes his family background giving his whole demeanour a majestic quality. He is true worshipper of God, and does so by kneeling before Him every morning and evening to seek His blessings. He is truly a great human being in every sense of the word.

My father must have been a terribly lonely person after the death of my mother, but he never expressed his deep sense of invaluable loss. He visits our mother's *Samadhi* everyday, where a beautiful cupola was constructed and places flowers on it. Five years later, after my grandmother's death, he had another *Samadhi* made and never forgets to place flowers on it as well. Incidentally both these *Samadhis* are close to our farmhouse, which was my mother's favourite spot from where she watched our fields. My father had her cremated on that very spot. Such was his love for his wife. Both cupolas over the *Samadhis* were designed by my younger brother whom I call *Naru*.

My Mother came from the *Royal* family of *Ratlam* (*M.P.*). I was really lucky to have an excellent mother, who strained every nerve for the welfare of her husband and children. In my ignorance, at time, I might have grumbled that my mother was too harsh and strict, but as I grew up, I realized why she did what she did and thank her profusely acknowledging the fact had it not been for her sternness, I wouldn't have been what I am today. She was a great lady and resolved every problem with rare wisdom. I was never sent to a boarding school. My disciplined upbringing by her carved out my life for which I'll remain eternally grateful to her. She passed away in January 1990 leaving a void in my life.

My Mother not only brought us up but also the children of my uncle Raj who grew up with us like the children in a joint family. Her younger brother died early leaving four children (two boys and two girls) behind at a very young age. My mother also helped my widowed aunt in every possible way in bringing up these children. They were given good education, after which both the boys started working and both the girls got married in respectable homes. She scarified a great deal to see to it that every one of them was provided with everything they needed.

Both my parents got along very well. They were an ideal couple. They gave us lots of love and security. They both coordinated their effort and raised their children as a team. Whenever we went to them with any demand or request, they communicated with each other through their eyes. We could never know how they decided things but we were always made to feel comfortable and wanted. I have a feeling that my father had a soft corner for me. Most of the time he favoured me, maybe because I was the only daughter who was 'destined' to go away from him after her marriage. But he never spoilt me. By and large, my parents were kind and loving, not only to their children but the other children as well. My father, on his retirement, did and is continuing to do even now a lot of social work for the welfare of poor people. He takes a lot of care of the needy in the village where he hails from, as a result of which these people virtually worship him.

Character Building: My parents put a lot of emphasis on character building of their children. My father reminded us constantly and I quote, "If you have lost money, you have lost nothing, if you have lost health, you have lost something, and if you have lost character, you have lost everything." The qualities that they did their best to drill into us were honesty, truthfulness and sincerity. My father also warned us not to get too close to anyone indiscriminately as most people were insensitive and completely indifferent to finer feelings. Thanks to them that freedom, self-reliance and love of adventure became my second nature.

My **elder brother Sangram Singh** is also handsome man like my father. He spent most of his childhood in a boarding school because of which I saw very little of him. He studied in St. Xaviers School, *Jaipur* till Sr. Cambridge and passed out as the Head Boy of the School. After finishing his B.A., he joined the Indian Army. He too was a very kind and loving person like my parents. He left army as a major after fourteen and half years of service. In fact he gave up when he was at the peak of his career to do something, which was closer to his heart. He wanted to spend most of his time with books and practise meditation. At the time he was posted to *Kaduna (Nigeria)* as an instructor in *Nigerian Military Academy*. Having served there for four years, he made up his mind to leave the army. It was his own decision. He got his last posting as an adjutant in the Indian Military Academy, Dehradun. After a year or so, once his papers were through, he left. My sister-in-law *Shakuntala*, a very sincere and devoted wife of his, stood by him. She herself, though academically highly qualified and a gold medalist from University is extremely competent and an ideal housewife. They have a son *Abhimanyu* who was hardly six years old when my brother left army. Now he is a grown up, handsome young man. He got married to a very pretty girl, *Priti*, two years ago. Now he is working and leading a happy married life in Delhi. Both my brother and sister-in-law are now living with my father at a farmhouse and taking very good care of him.

My **younger brother**, **Narendra Singh**, became a successful exporter of leather garments after graduating from college. After about 20 years he sold his business and became a hotelier. Today he owns a beautiful hotel in Jaipur. He is also deeply involved in charitable work and looks after various projects for the welfare of Rajput community. Following in the footsteps of my father, he too is doing a lot to help the poor, illiterate, helpless widows and war widows. Most of his charitable work is devoted to backward villages and smaller towns. His wife Harsh too shares his work. They have a lovely daughter, *Chavvi*, who has done her M.B.A. and is now working.

My **uncle Raj Singh** has always been like a friend to us. He also used to participate in various games we children enjoyed playing during our younger days. My father always admonished him saying that he was yet to grow up. With our uncle on our side, we could get away with anything. He took us to movies, picnics, boating, eating out in restaurants. In fact I use to cry after he would leave to go back to his job. I missed him so much that I would stop listening to music or radio and that went on for days together. He was the life and soul of our house. He was very fond of good food. My mother and aunt *Rama* always prepared lovely dishes for him. Actually my mother was an excellent housewife and a great cook. My aunt learnt a lot from her and became as proficient as my mother. They both lived like sisters and gave a lot of respect to each other.

My father, both my brothers and their wives are like a huge shady tree. Anyone can sit under it and relax.

Hari Singh and his wife *Ragini* are running a beautiful high school. They have two grown up and handsome sons - *Nardeep* and *Vishvender.* Hari and Ragini takes very good care of uncle and aunt and live with them. Ragini is a great cook. Food at her place is always a treat.

Vijay Singh and his wife *Prakash* live in *Bombay.* Vijay is doing business over there. They have two lovely children, a girl and a boy, *Natasha* and *Avi.* Natasha is older while *Avi* is a couple of years younger. Last I heard from them is that after their schooling in the *U.S.A.,* they have come back to their parents in *Bombay* to pursue their studies.

Lt. Col. Ajay Singh and his wife, *Meenakshi* are in Cochin in *Kerala.* Ajay is still serving in the Army. He plans to settle down in Jaipur after his retirement. They have a small son *Dhruv* who is studying in school.

My husband, Dev, was born on 27th August 1941 in **Udaipur** in the family of *Ranawats,* who are direct descendants of the great warrior *Maharan Pratap,* thus belonging to the ruling family of *Mewar.* He comes from an affluent and educated, rather large family of *Kakerwa,* a village in the erstwhile princely state of *Udaipur.* His father *Mr. Bhawani Singh Ranawat* was an officer in the administrative service, but unfortunately died when Dev was still in high school. His uncle *Mr. Jawan Singh Ranawat*, who was then the Chief Justice of Rajasthan then took him under his wing and became his mentor. Another uncle of his, *Mr. Mahender Singh Ranawat*, was a member for the first *Rajya Sabha* of Independent India. His eldest uncle, *Thakur Saheb of Kakerwa*, was a noble soul who stayed back in their ancestral village and took care of his land and property and his kith and kin like a father.

Dev loved *shikar* (hunting) and it happened to be his favourite hobby. When I got married to him, I too accompanied him for shikar and enjoyed it, but later I developed a kind of repulsion for it and tried to stop him, but he did not listen to me. I resented his shikari friends for taking him out on shoots, but it was none of their fault. Dev went with them willingly and enjoyed doing so. Later when a law prohibiting shooting was passed, I locked up his guns. Thank God for that! But at times his urge for a 'shoot' was so overwhelming that many a time he virtually implored me saying, "Mama, please let me shoot, my soul lies in shooting, who am I to kill any creature, it only happens with the will of God Almighty. Not a leaf moves without his consent." I would always say to him, "You are hurting so many souls. So what if they are animals! You are destroying nature, so please stop it. You are not going anywhere. Go and play golf." Dev always held that against me.

Dev and I have ultimately decided to settle in *Jaipur* and built our house here. We first built our house in *Poona* being a neutral territory, because neither of us belonged to this place. Moreover, both Dev and I liked Poona very much and wanted to settle down there. Later due to my prolonged stay in *Jaipur* (because of my work), we built a house there. But before doing so I had asked Dev if he would like to stay in *Jaipur*, as he was a native of *Udaipur*. He said, "Yes, I like this place and love your people who are so nice and respectful towards me." His answer touched my heart. Yes! My family really loves him. It is nice to be with people around who give so much of love and make you feel wanted. Most of the time, we have lots of fun and throw parties. Whenever we are together, our place comes alive with laughter. I myself laugh a lot and keep provoking others to do so. I am easily put off by people who do not know how to laugh. I feel sorry for them. They are the ones who are losers in life.

Jaipur is a place where my maternal and paternal uncles and aunts live because of which we receive a lot of love from them. Another very interesting thing is that *Jaipur* is Mecca of Polo. This is my favourite sport and I love watching it.

Dev has always been a great source of strength and has always held my hand in time of need. I needed his love and understanding in order to grow and explore the world, something that became the most important part of my life. I am really grateful to Dev in helping me become more and more aware of the world.

Ronilla, my daughter, has been like a friend ever since she grew up. We always shared all our problems and hid nothing from each other. Even as a youngster, she was mature for her age and very understanding. She never gave any trouble to us. She was a boon and a blessing for us. At school she was good in her studies and excelled both in sports and dramatics. She was an all rounder who did well in anything she took up. She was very young when she was married off to *Dr. Pritipal Singh*, who saw my daughter in her final year in school as a boarder. *Pritipal* who was then studying in a medical college in Karachi was smitten by her beauty and behaviour. He happened to be the son of *Rana Chander Singh of Umarkot* (*Amarkot*), the ruler of a *Rajput state* now in *Pakistan*. After the partition in 1947, this state became part of Pakistan. At the time *Rana Arjun Singh*, father of *Rana Chander Singh* was asked if he would like his state to be a part of Pakistan or India. He preferred Umarkot to be a part of Pakistan because geographically it was a part of the *Sindh* province. All their lands were irrigated by a canal where the family was used to living like feudal lords. They still have a very big land holding. Rana Chander Singh has always been active in politics. He spent 53 years of his life as a member of National Assembly of Pakistan and had been, from time to time, a federal Minister for Agriculture, Narcotics, Revenue and the Chairman of National Commission of minorities for a number of years in Pakistan. He always won election as an independent candidate - a very credible thing for a *Hindu* (*Rajput*) living in Pakistan. Apart from his sound standing in politics, he is worshipped by his people in Umarkot. He has a tremendous personality and is a man of great character. His mother, *Dev Kumari*, is nearly 92 years, but amazingly full of life even now. She is an institution in herself. His wife, *Rani Sahiba Subhdra*, too is a wonderful person and a very devoted wife and a mother. There are lots of *Rajputs* living across the border, who are more traditional in their outlook than the Rajputs living in India. His eldest son *Hamir Singh* is active in politics now. He too was member of the provincial assembly for a number of years and was the minister of science and technology in state of Sindh. One of his sons *Bhopal Singh* married and settled in *U.S.A.* It is this family to which Dr. Pritipal Singh belongs to. He and my daughter Ronilla are happily married couple. Rana's daughter *Sangeeta* is married here, in Jaipur. The marriage took place in India because it is customary amongst the Rajputs not to marry in the same clan. They being *Sodda Rajputs* had to find someone from a different clan. Rana Chander Singh and his wife mostly lived in Islamabad because of Rana's involvement in politics. The fort of Umarkot has been taken over by the Government. The *Rana Jagir* is 16 km from Umarkot Fort. It has a great historical value because Akbar the great was born in the Umarkot Fort. His father, *Humayun* was on the run after being defeated by *Shershah Suri* when he was given refuge by the then Rana of Umarkot. At the time *Hamida Bano*, Humayun's wife was in the last stages of her pregnancy, and gave birth to Akbar the Great in Umarkot.

The following write up appeared in Pakistan Newspaper 'The Nation' on Thursday 9th November, 1989

Rehoboam______________Ardeshir Cowasjee

Rana Chandarsingh of Umarkot, a five-time member of what is erroneously referred to as our respected and august National Assembly, this time around, pledged his initial support to the Pakistan Peoples Party. As time went by, day by day, disillusion set in and the Rana, being a candid out-spoken man, did not conceal his dissatisfaction with the manner in which the country, and his province in particular, were not being governed by the Government; what little confidence he had was soon effectively eroded.

The Rana of Umarkot, feeling perhaps like so many others, that anything, however disorganized, was still better than what was, pledged, together with some of his Sindhi Compatriots, to support the no-confidence motion. They were reportedly asked to swear their allegiance by all that was holy and the Rana's fellow dissenters duly performed on the Book. He, when asked to swear by *Geeta*, suggested that God be left undisturbed and in peace in his heaven and not be involved in the murky affairs of Islamabad. His word, the word of a Rajput, was his bond and he, on earth, would abide by that word come hell or high water. His word was indeed his bond and it held; that of the others, later proved to be worthless.

The Press, the vernacular Press in particular, has scathingly condemned the ignominy and abasement of the Rana's co-members and to him have given great credit for his unusual act-unusual by our standards that is – of keeping his word. Perhaps the finest disapprobation was *MILLAT's* editorial on November 5, (*Sharam Nivaat*), the writer of which, a gold-medialist in Gujarati proficiency, deserves to be congratulated. He pities the majority for having to be taught by the minority what it is that uprightness stands for.

The history of Umarkot, the fortress town on the edge of the great *Thar Desert*, is replete with tales of the steadfast courage of its Rajput Ranas. In August 1542, Humayun, his young Sindhi consort and his followers, accompanied by only seven armed horsemen, sought refuge in Umarkot. Rana Parshad received the starving and thirsty fugitives with generous hospitality, providing them with all that was necessary. On October 15, (447 years and 2 days ago) was born *Abu-ul-Fath Jalal-ud-din Mohammad*

Akbar, later to become the greatest of the *Mughal Emperors of India*. A descendant of *Parshad, Rana Rattansingh, Aam-mukhtiar* (prime minister) to the *Talpur Mirs*, was shot by one of *Napier's Generals*, Tyrwhitt, for refusing to break his oath of fidelity to the *Talpurs*. In 1946, Chandar Singh's father, Arjun Singh, made a promise to the Muslim League to contest an election as an associate member against the Congress candidate. *Swami Krishnanand*, did not yield to *Nehru's* persuasion when he came all the way to Umarkot to see him. It was unfortunate that Arjun died before the day of the election.

The list is long and all men of good thought will undoubtedly share the hope that Rana Chandar Singh is left to follow the dictates of his conscience (a very rare commodity these days) and that neither he nor any member of his family and followers are victimized or harassed by our political bully-boys. The message to the bullies (who by their very nature are cowards), to the red, black or green-shirted street gangs, should be that Rana Chandar Singh as read, heard or known of, is a man of substance — in his case substance is not indicative of sugar mills, cotton gins or high-rise buildings. Being a man of such substance, he is worth having on any decent side.

Ronilla has two nice looking sons *Shiv Karan Singh*, who is going to be nine years old, and *Bhawani Singh*, who is seven-and-a-half years old. Ronilla is now the Administrative Coordinator of seventeen schools in Karachi and Hyderabad known as *Foundation Public Schools*. Dr. Pritipal Singh is now working as a doctor in *Aga Khan Hospital* in Karachi. Their whole family lives together in *Karachi*. I feel good seeing my child taking care of every body in the joint family, looking after her children and husband. She is a very good mother and a devoted wife. But what really goes to her credit is that all the principals of these seventeen schools, Directors who work with her in the Head Office and the owners of the school Mr. and *Mrs. Minhas* are all praise for her. Mr. and Mrs. Minhas wanted to see both my husband and me and called us to their place for a lavish tea party. Every delicacy one could think of was there to eat. How hospitable Pakistanis are! One has to see it to believe it! We both were very touched when they said, "We wanted to see you both because we wanted to find out what stock our girl came from? She has a heart of gold and works very hard with great involvement and commitment. She can practically handle everything competently. We can say that because we have watched her since she joined us as a young bride." They were very happy with her performance. In between Ronilla and Dr. Pritipal went away to U.S.A. (Michigan) for four years. Dr. Pritipal did his Master's Degree in hospital administration after which they came back. It was during this time she had her babies and once they grew up she went back to her job. The whole family lives in Karachi and all the festivals are celebrated at Umarkot. Menfolk make several visits to take care of lands.

My son Rohit, like his sister, was very close to me. He grew up to be a sincere, truthful and a genuine person. He was peace-loving and kept away from trouble. Whenever he had any problem, he confided in me and paid need to my guidance. In fact as a very young boy, whenever he had fever, he immediately swallowed any bitter medicine I gave him. He was such an obedient child! He being younger of my two children was the apple of my eye. He went to *Mayo College, Ajmer* as a boarder at a very young age, when he was hardly eight and remained there till he finished high school. Afterwards he joined St. Stephens College in Delhi. There he earned his master's degree and straight away joined J. Thomas in Calcutta, tea tasting and a tea auctioning company. He worked there for almost three years and then decided to quit. During that time, I loved going to Calcutta and staying with my son. He was enjoying a high standard of living, with a flat and a car and servants at his disposal. He took me around to famous restaurants, clubs and also to the city's golf course and squash club. When I first went there, Rohit had just won the Inter Tea Companies Squash Championship that year. Anyway after visiting him twice, I liked the company for which he worked and advised him not to leave it. But he disagreed with me saying that his soul does not find happiness in that kind of work. So he resigned, came to Delhi and joined an American fitness company. Fitness line was one in which his soul revelled.

As the luck would have it, he met ***Giulia***, his future wife, who was also posted in Delhi during this period. They first met each other at a common friend's house. Giulia was then working as a legal officer in *United Nations High Commission for Refugees*. Rohit had confided in me that he would marry only when he finds a soul mate. Otherwise he would always remain single. So I should not look for a girl for him till he gives me a green signal. So I never brought up the subject and meanwhile he had found Giulia. Giulia's mother, *Hildegard*, was a *German*, and her father, Francesco, was an Italian. She had lost her father at a young age, just before coming to Delhi. She cried whenever her father's name came up. Her beautiful mother was a large-hearted, hospitable and a great lady. We became very good friends after their marriage. Giulia had inherited good qualities from both her mother and father. She is extremely nice and a loving human being. In fact I have learnt a lot from her. She is mature, dignified and a cool person with lots of patience, with no desires or craving for anything. She seems to be a person who is complete in herself. They had a court marriage in *Geneva* and later had an Indian wedding here in Jaipur and again a church wedding in *Europe Boxmeer*. I can never forget her family and friends, who came flying from all over the world! We all stayed in a Hotel. I had never seen a hotel with such exquisite environment located beautifully on a bank of a lake and in the midst of semi wilderness. Theirs is a very close-knit family like our own. Her grand mother called *Oma,* who passed away at the age of 92 in 2003 was again a grand old lady. I enjoyed visiting her a number of times in *Germany*. She had a lakeside house where she spent summer and winter in a warm winter-house. Their hospitality was simply incomparable. Between Giulia's mother in Boxmeer and grandmother in Germany, we were really pampered in everyway. Both of them had wonderfully done up magnificent houses. Hildegard, Giulia's mother passed away in September 2004. She could never forget her husband and the pain of having been separated from him probably took her away too soon. Her desire was to be buried next to her husband which was fulfilled by both her children. Giulia's brother, *Stephno,* is a pilot and a Captain with the British Airways. His wife *Sabini* and two little girls *Elena* and *Isabella* are very pretty.

After their marriage in December 1998, Giulia and Rohit got posted in *Geneva (Switzerland)*. On the 12th of June 2002, they were blessed with a cute baby boy. Their son Francesco Vijay Singh Ranawat (rather a long name) is three years old now whom I call "Lopchoo". He can understand & speak four languages i.e. English, German, Nepali & Hindi. He is a very intelligent boy. His mother Giulia is a linguist and speaks five languages – *German, French, Italian, English* & *Spanish.* After completing four years they were posted to *Nepal.* But wherever they may be, we keep in close touch and often visit each other.

Apart from all that, I have a distinct memory of a few things about both my son Rohit and daughter Ronilla that I cherish.

Rohit was always very cautious by nature - whenever we all went to see off Dev at the railway station, he insisted that Dev should stand inside the compartment and only then talk to us. We tried telling him on a number of occasions not to worry as Dev was usually the sole passenger in the 1st class compartment (during those days), and could hop in as soon as the whistle blew, but he never liked the idea. He hated to see anyone getting into a moving train.

*****

He loved people who were gentle. The first school he went to, his class teacher was not very kind towards him because of which he did not like to go to her class, but since we had insisted he should go there, Rohit would simply sit on the steps outside but never went back to the classroom. This went on for a week or so when we finally decided not to send him to that school.

*****

We had him admitted into another school. He loved the class teacher and never missed the class even for a single day. After a couple of months, he had measles with high temperature and his doctor asked him not to go to school for a week or so. Now it was a problem for us to keep him home. He kept howling and insisted to be taken to his school. Both Dev and I took him there in our car. Dev went in and talked to his class teacher explaining the situation to her while I stayed with Rohit in the car. *Mrs. Sheereen Omer*, his class teacher, an understanding and an affectionate person by nature, came outside and told Rohit to go back home since she would be away to *Bombay* for ten days and there would be no one to take care of him in the class. Rohit straightaway agreed and we drove back home.

*****

On one of Dev's postings in Meerut, we kept a small dog. During summer, we used to sleep in the open, in the back of our house, inside the mosquito nets, with table fans on. This was the *'in thing'* at that time. We noticed that at bedtime, Rohit would quietly put his slippers under his mattress because the dog had already chewed up a pair of his tiny slippers. After the incident, he became very careful as not lose his pair of slippers once again. At that time, he was hardly three. I found it very amusing.

*****

Dev's sister's husband, though bald, had very hairy hands! Rohit always watched him carefully and then one day when he could not resist, he asked him, "Uncle, why did you remove your hair from your head and put them all over your hands? You should not have done a thing like that!"

*****

Rohit was hardly eight and half when he went to the boarding school at Mayo College. He hated being away from the family. That is why we called him "a family man" because he always missed us all and wrote lovely letters. Once while going back to school after holidays he said to me, "Mama, I wish I can make you a Tom Thumb and carry you in my pocket wherever I go. While attending the classes, you can be locked up in my cupboard; it's a very safe place." I was really touched. Every time holidays were just about to end, he would count days, hours and minutes and say to me, "You are the best mother in the world and yet you let me go back like this". As I sit back and think now, I feel how strong I must have been at that time as to insist on his going back to the Boarding school for his own good.

*****

Being in the Army, Rohit hardly saw his father while growing up due to frequent field postings. So whenever Dev came on leave, he would come running to me and say, "Mama, look that nice uncle has come back to our house." I would say, "No, he is your daddy and not uncle." But he could not understand. He would feel shy for a couple of days and then make friends with his father. Growing up in the absence of a parent is hard on growing children.

*****

Both Rohit and sister Ronilla accompanied me for riding everyday. I left them both with the instructor. At that time they were three and seven years old respectively. Ronilla being older rode well but Rohit always looked sleepy and tired while riding. When I'd return after an hour, his instructor would laugh and tell me that Rohit falls asleep even while riding. I told him I was not surprised because he falls asleep while eating and especially while chewing a bone!

*****

Ronilla, my daughter being our first child and also being the first grand child in my and Dev's family, was very pampered and naughty but in a healthy way.

While going on one of our weekend trips in Shillong, our jeep had a headlong collision with a bus while climbing up the hills. The jeep got damaged badly but we got saved. At the time Ronilla was hardly two-years old. She got off, took a stick and started hitting the bus saying, "Why did you hit our jeep?" Both my husband and I were impressed with her defiant gesture.

*****

Once a balloon seller came near our house, for the first time, and kids from the neighbourhood surrounded him. Ronilla who was inside the house with the maid also saw him from the compound and ran outside without being noticed by any one of us. She followed the balloon seller. He too had no clue as to which house she came from! The maid started howling when she saw the little one was missing. We all rushed in different directions of the road outside our house. For the next half an hour we looked for her, anxiously, and when we found her, she was merrily chirping away with the balloon man when she could barely talk! Thank God she was not very far from our home. She was thrilled when we bought a lot of balloons for her.

*****

During this time she used to go riding on a horse's back, early in the morning. The *syais* would take her around and while returning home she always asked him to stop at a particular point where a pan shop (prepared out of a leaf) was located. She would ask for a pan. The shop was hardly open that early in the morning, but she always came home chewing a pan. Later, after a couple of years we went to attend a wedding. There she did not eat anything. When I asked her why, she said, "I had twenty pans". Actually, the wedding party next to the dining area arranged a pan stall so that people could enjoy the pan after dinner. She noticed the stall on arrival and stuffed herself with all the pans she could. Now that she is grown up she still enjoys a pan.

*****

During summer vacations, in case my parents were there, I always took the kids to my parent's farmhouse at Jaipur. The farm's caretaker had seven small children of my children's age. Ronilla was more like a tomboy. She was out the whole day in the fields playing with these children indulging in pranks with them. Both the kids enjoyed their holidays to the fullest and always talked of those days as "our best holidays" for being left all by themselves to do whatever they liked and to be closer to the nature which they really enjoyed.

*****

When Ronilla was in the 11th grade, she opted for science subjects because I had requested her to do so. After a month or so when I visited her again, she had dark circles under eyes. When I asked her the reason she said, "See this is what science has given me." We both laughed at her comment, but then I told her to drop science and take arts.

*****

Dev never liked anyone crying in his presence. So Ronilla was too asked not to do that right from her early childhood days. She adhered to it quite strictly. After her marriage, when I was seeing her and my son-in-law off, I burst into tears. When a daughter leaves the house, after being a part of it for all those years, it is difficult for any mother not to cry. That moment was the most heart breaking for me. Even now when I see any daughter leaving her parents home and going to her in-laws home, I break down no matter who the girl is. At the time when I hugged Ronilla, she said, "Mama, please don't cry. I don't know how to cry." She had certainly become a strong girl, something that I realized on that day only. In no time my tears vanished.

*****

Ronilla's two sons, her elder son, Karan, has reached an age when he has begun to understand everything but the younger one is yet to grow up, and is more sensitive by nature. Now if I cry, when they are ready to go back after the holidays, he always asks his mother if someone has hurt his grandma, and if someone has, he is not going to spare that person.

3
Spiritual Journey

Life is a strange admixture of pain and pleasure. Mine has been no exception. My spiritual journey started in 1980 when I decided to follow all the major religions of the world. I spent two to three years on each of them. Being a *Hindu* myself, I practiced *Buddhism* for two years, *Christianity* for three years, *Islam* for two years and then turned to universal spiritualism - the doctrine that spirit is the ultimate reality. I feel spiritualism is truly a world religion today and that is what I believe in now.

Now let me go back and narrate some important events in my life. I was married on the 22nd June 1965 when I was only seventeen years old. On the morning of 23rd June, my parents sent my husband Dev and me to a temple of Goddess *Shila Devi* at *Amber*, the old capital of *Jaipur*, which is very close to the Jaipur city where we lived. This goddess happened to be our family deity. I prayed to goddess Shila Devi to bless us for a happy married life. On 24th June we were given a send off and we departed for *Udaipur* by car. On our way to *Udaipur* we broke our journey to get blessings of a saint, known as *Data Maharaj*, who was the patron saint of my in-laws. I still have a loving picture of his in my mind. His blessings have always been with me. Today when I sit back I realize how he blessed me from the core of his heart. I think he must have been the first person who initiated me in the search for God. Today I thank Data Maharaj from the core of my heart. At that time I had no clue of the impact his blessings were going to make to my future.

As a little girl, whenever I went to my father's village, I always made it a point to visit different temples in the evenings along with my village friends. I loved village life that was situated by the side of a lake. We'd take some flour mixed with sugar for the ants and sprinkle it around ants' holes in the fields. I have a feeling that ants were happy whenever we approached them. In the evening as the dusk fell, all the girls, including myself, observed silence for half an hour. I still wonder how could we, as little girls, keep quite for so long. My village friends taught all those things to me. But it is only now that I realize the meaning of what we did. That's why I observe silence while meditating even today and keep food (millets) and water for birds and ants in my garden everyday. Everything that we learn as a child has a meaning. That is why when I grew up I visited most of the famous temples of India and *Nepal* and also the churches and *cathedrals, mosques* and *monasteries* abroad.

Even in my early childhood, I felt the presence of God, because I always felt He was not far away, but somewhere very close to me. I especially felt His presence every time I was waging a battle to overcome some extremely difficult situation in my life. At times like that, something miraculous always happened to support me when I was about to fall. He would send some stranger to lend me a helping hand, after which I hardly ever met him. Whenever some people went all out to crush me, help always came to me through a noble human being. How can I ever forget those beautiful hands, which came to my rescue? Similarly in times of great joy and happiness I felt His presence in the same way. One never sees the power or spirit, which responds to your prayers in times of need, but only feels its presence. Those who have received His grace are blessed. These incidents made me search for Him, and once I set out on that path, there was no going back. I firmly believe that God too wants us to know Him, feel Him and love Him. Here I would like to relate an incident, which strengthened my faith in Him.

In September 1989, I went to *Jammu and Kashmir* with a couple of my friends. At that time Dev was posted in a forward area known as *Kupwara.* The families were allowed to visit the place only at a specified time in summer. It happened to be a very beautiful valley close to the Lolab valley. Some parts of Lolab valley reminded me of Switzerland which I had first visited in May 1981. Jammu & Kashmir has some of the most beautiful places in India. While going around, the feeling of being so close to nature was simply sublime. After visiting most of the places, which are worth seeing in Jammu & Kashmir, we decided to see *Amarnath.* It is one of the holiest and oldest temples in India. It is located at a great height amidst the icy mountains. You have either to walk or go there on Ponies. It is an arduous journey. One has to climb steep hilly areas. According to a legend, Lord Shiva – the creator, preserver and destroyer - resides here with his wife goddess Parvati. It is one of the two most worshipped places of Lord Shiva. The other one is in Nepal (*Kathmandu*) known as *Pashupati Nath Temple.* Today Nepal is the only nation state in the world, which professes and practices Hinduism.

At that point of my life I was still not sure about which religion I should follow. Starting from a place known as *Baltal,* we reached this most beautiful place. A feeling of tranquillity and peace of mind overwhelmed me. It had tremendous aura of divinity.

I felt God was somewhere very close to me. It was then that I sincerely prayed, "Oh! Lord wherever you are, please help me in finding You. Please listen to me and show me the way to reach you." Yes, I am convinced that He did - that was something I realized only after my return to Jaipur.

Here I must relate an incident, which strengthened my faith in God. It so happened that after our group of friends had left the temple and traversed quite a distance, when I suddenly realized that my handbag was missing. It had my camera, an important diary and diary of telephone numbers and addresses, cash and keys of the suitcases and some other tit-bits. While visiting a Hindu temple or shrine it is a customary thing to leave the shoes outside at some distance in the care of some people and walk bare-feet to the temple. What happened was that one of my friends had taken my handbag while I was removing my shoes. The handbag was a bit heavy. Thoughtfully he kept holding it for me so that I could pray better, by not having anything in my hands.

On our way back we were all too engrossed in talking to each other that I didn't notice this friend of ours who was left far behind us. As he came closer, I asked him where was my bag, because he did not have anything in his hand. He told me he had placed it next to me while I was wearing my shoes. It was my fault because I took it for granted that it must be with him. Now the question was how to recover it. Thousands of people must have come and gone from the shoe corner outside of the temple. It was very cold and slippery with snow all around. Our friend then volunteered to go back and bring the bag in case some body had still not taken it away. I told him that I had faith that it would still be there, as it is being taken care of by Lord Shiva. Usually handbags are not found and get stolen. Our friend came back with the bag and told us that the bag was lying uncrushed and safe, in the midst of that huge crowd where it was difficult to even put a toe. For me it was an indication that Lord Shiva had heard my prayers. I laughed and thanked Him. It was from here that my spiritual journey began.

It is most amazing, the house where I was born and the one in which I am now living are on the same road, only this one is much further down the road. I pass my childhood home everyday. The house in which we are now residing was made about seventeen years ago. One could call it a country home. It is a very quiet place far away from the din and noise of city life. My husband and I love it. Being in the army, my husband often got posted to non-family stations because of which I had to supervise its construction work until it was completed. Being very far from the town, it entailed a lot of running around. It was certainly quite difficult to handle the labour. However, I followed the dictum: Never say die! And carried on. There was practically nothing around at that time except a very small two-room house with lot of open space around it. An old lady named Bhagawani Devi lived there. At that time she was more than seventy years old. Every morning, before dawn, I went out for a jog and crossed the place. The old lady lived all alone in the wilderness. Occasionally we wished each other and that was all. Once or twice, I did feel that she wanted to talk to me but I was always in a hurry to get back and take care of the construction work and my business.

One Sunday, I halted at her place. We talked about each other's life. She told me that the place where she was living belonged to her Master. It was an Ashram. "What does your master do?" I asked. "He travels all over the world and gives knowledge to people", she said. "What does knowledge mean?" I asked. She said, "It is an art of going within oneself and contacting your soul, which is sole source of your energy". "What happens when you contact this energy or soul?" I asked her. "We come to know that we are a spark of same divine light." "But how do we imbibe this knowledge." Her answer was: "Through prayer." I came away and forgot about it. On the following Sunday, she came to my place and asked me if I would allow her to watch television every Sunday morning because a very nice programme, based on Indian religious book known as "*Mahabharat*" was being telecast at that time. "You certainly can, but I can only offer you my bedroom as the rest of the house is incomplete," I told her. She gladly accepted and watched the programme. I too sat down with her and started watching it and found it to be very interesting. In between we also talked of her Master and his grace on her. This went on for a number of months and then she stopped coming. I too got busy because of Dev who was on leave for a month and my son who also came down from his college in *Delhi*. After almost two to three weeks, I went to her place and found that she was in the hospital. There was another lady who had taken her place in the Ashram. After finding out the address of the hospital, we both, Dev and I visited her. She was calm and serene and was very happy to see us. She had cancer of the uterus, but the unfortunate part was that there was no arrangement for chemotherapy as the hospital's machine was non functional. Being poor, she couldn't afford to go anywhere else. She had lost her husband at a young age, she had two sons from him. She had brought them up. Luckily they acquired good jobs and were happily married with children. But unfortunately, later, her younger son died leaving his young wife and children. The elder son's wife too passed away after a couple of years leaving behind her children. She was badly shaken by these painful tragedies, but despite everything her faith in her Master remained unshakable. Once her grandchildren grew up, she left her family and dedicated her life to her Master and his work. She took care of the Ashram and whenever there were programmes in the Ashram she supervised everything. The main Ashram of the Master was in *Delhi*. Programmes for thousands of people, who flocked there from all over India were conducted twice a year. Some time more than one lakh people attended the programme. The Master himself visited for about four days flying in from abroad, in order to instruct the people. The programme always lasted for three days. *Bhagawani Devi* personally attended these programmes during which she experienced a feeling of total bliss in presence of her Master.

Since she was out of touch with her family, I took charge of her and the medical attention required for her. I sent her off to *Bikaner* where everything was available for her treatment. We arranged a nice person to escort her and stay with her during the treatment. This person who went with her too was happy, being a devotee of the same Master.

When she returned, she was looking better. Despite chemotherapy there was a glow on her face. It was the faith in her Master, which did wonders. She was all right, she ate well and was healthy again. One day, all of a sudden, she fell sick again.

I made it a point to go and see her everyday. Actually she again needed hospitalisation, but by this time she told me that her time had come and she must go. She was in the hospital only for a couple of days when the doctor told us that her end was near - she could go home. I tried to look after her as well as I could with all the resources at my disposal. At the time she made me promise two things. One was that I must receive this knowledge and the other was to visit the Master in *Delhi* whenever the next programme took place. One day much before she passed away, she confided in me that she often talked to her Master in her dreams. Next time when I went to see her she told me that the Master had come in her dream again, to see as to where she was residing. At that time she told her Master, "I am living in this far off place, which is far away from town. Now that I have fallen sick, where is the doctor?" And then she saw me standing next to the Master. Pointing at me the Master said that this is your doctor and assured her that from thereon she'd look after you. I didn't say anything to her but thought to myself that it must have been some superior power, which made my husband and me visit the elderly woman in the hospital and guided us to look after her.

Just as her soul was leaving her body, she said to me, "You must have been my daughter in my past life. I must go. The Master has come to take me away." She closed her eyes and passed away peacefully. It was a true relationship between the Master and the devotee. I too could feel his presence. This touched my heart in such a way that I too made a firm decision to gain this knowledge. She had been my true friend in every way. A couple of days before her death, an instructor (Mahatma ji) came from *Delhi Ashram* to enquire about Bhagwani Devi's health. She had requested him to teach me the knowledge of going within. He being an instructor could easily do so. His name is *Dineshanand ji.* But at the same time I wasn't mentally prepared to receive it.

After Bhagwani Devi's death I felt very low and decided to visit Dev for a fortnight along with some of our friends. There in the temple of *Amarnath* my prayer was heard. When I came back, the same instructor came again. We fixed to meet. It was the day of *Diwali* - the day when this festival of lights is celebrated all over India! A great Indian festival! That was the day when Maharaj ji became my guru, my Master.

MY MASTER

Maharaj ji to his disciples: Prem Pal Singh Rawat, was born on Indian soil on December 10, 1957 in *Kankhal* village off the holy city of *Haridwar.* Tutored by his father *Hansji Maharaj* as a little boy, Maharaj-ji began his discourses when he was barely six years of age.

Even though the youngest of his four sons, Hansji Maharaj had noticed *Prempal's* spiritual leanings and wanted him to be his successor. When Maharaj ji lost his father in 1966, he was barely nine years old. According to the wishes of his Master, he not only became his successor but also vowed to spread knowledge of exploring innermost consciousness the world over. He went abroad for the first time in 1971 and ever since people from all over the world have gained from his teachings and discourses. During his trips to India, usually once in six months, he imparts amazing knowledge in search of Him within oneself. His discourses are often translated into 65 languages to reach the maximum number of people everywhere.

One's guru has special place in one's life. No one could illustrate this better than *Kabir*, one of the greatest saints of his time:

"My *Guru* (Master) and my God are standing together,

Whom should I prostrate to first?

The Master first because it is through the Master, the God has been shown to me."

As a child, even though I had heard about conscience, inner voice, instinct, sixth sense and intuition, the meaning was unclear to me. Later, I also started raising such questions: Why am I here? What is the purpose of human existence? It is only now that I realize that the sole purpose of life is to experience divinity which otherwise would lie dormant within us and the only answer to this is spirituality. And it is for this purpose alone that one needs a spiritual preceptor. A human being must evolve. It is a process of inner cleansing. Just as we keep our surroundings – our homes, rooms – clean, so we should clean our hearts so that God resides in it.

Once I was taught the technique of going within I started practicing meditation everyday. After three months my Master came to Delhi. My whole family namely, my husband, Dev, my son, daughter and myself went for his discourse. I was lucky because I was able to not only watch him at close quarters but also talk to him. Perhaps it was because my connection with him went back to the time of Bhagwani Devi's death. I distinctly recall the aroma of spray, which was used by me in her room, when she was sick. As the luck would have it, the same fragrance was sprayed in the room by an elderly lady where we sat waiting for my Master along with three or four more people. It was then that I heard my Master saying, "During the time of death, it's only your Master who's with you and no one else." In other words, it is nothing else except your own soul. He says just go wherever it takes you without any hesitation. I remember I had felt His presence at the time of the old lady's death. The truth is that a Master simply gives you the key to open your hearts. Guru is the one who leads you from darkness to light. But what is ordained by one's destiny has to happen.

The more I tried to concentrate my mind to reach the innermost depths of my being, the greater was my suffering. But the stings of misfortunes made me stronger. I began to detach myself from worldly relationships and desires realizing that bliss lay in discovering yourself by going deeper and deeper within. And it is there that you find an ocean of love, peace and contentment: all within you. Tap it and it will change your life for the better. Achieve that and a fountain of wisdom starts flowing within you. Nothing else changes but your outlook undergoes a complete transformation. The darkness disappears and you see only light.

On 16th January 1990 my mother passed away. She suffered a heart attack and within moments she was gone. When she lived she often said that her death would be painless and she would pass away without giving any trouble to anybody in her old age. She always wished to die before my father. Her wish came true. She was only sixty-two years of age. The cremation took place in the evening. That night when I sat down to meditate it was past midnight. I was overwhelmed by grief. I closed my eyes and going deep within myself asked my inner light, "Where has my mother gone to? Lord! Please show me where now she is." I experienced the most beautiful and mysterious thing in my life.

My Master who had heard my anguished cry showed me a large house, which was located on a hill. The type of house I envisioned is to be found only in the hill stations. They have sloping roofs with red tiles. The house had large gates and I saw my mother walking in. This experience made me realize further that my Master was within me. And it was He who made me go through this wonderful experience. I am sure if I ever come across this house, I'd recognize it straightaway. The difference between a Master and Nature is that Nature is indifferent and operates in its own way but Master cares and looks after His devotees. What does Master do? Master removes the *samskar* and brings out the real Self. Like a sculpture removes the dross and brings out a statue: like a master-craftsman chiselling a masterpiece. Spiritual evolution is a journey toward one's own liberation. It is a beautiful plane when everything becomes clear. A stage when your soul guides you through each minute of your existence.

Awareness of self (*Atman*) and God (*Parmatman*) is a special faculty given to human beings only. The role of master, Guru or preceptor is to guide you to go deep within yourself to realize that *Atman* is in fact a part of that *Parmatman*. The only thing that separates *Atman* from *Parmatman* is Maya, the diverse world as perceived by senses to conceal the unity of the Absolute Being. The very process of one's spiritual evolution involves seeing or becoming conscious of the deeper reality and removing the curtain of ignorance that blocks reality beyond Maya. When this realization dawns, then begins one's spiritual evolution and a person shuns ego. Along the path, one becomes emotionally stronger, fearless, confident, shedding hatred, greed and jealousy, which are life's inherent pitfalls. A true Guru or Master, as pointed out, is the one who after your initiation, takes you on the path of spiritual evolution. When one comes across such a Master, one experiences, instinctively, an aura around him and one's heart yearns for Him and one's whole being is swept with love and blissful contentment. Such a spiritually evolved person has the capacity to sow seeds of faith in human beings. This seed, when it blossoms, will liberate one from greed, hatred and fear. It is only through such Masters that one develops thirst and hunger to know the Creator.

In the Ramayana, rated as one of the holiest epics of India, Lord *Rama*, exiled for fourteen long years along with his wife *Sita* and younger brother *Laxman* made it a point to go out of their way, while passing through jungles and mountains to call on some of the *Maharishis*, saints and sages in order to show their reverence and imbibe wisdom from those who had scaled immense heights of spiritual evolution. One day *Laxman* asked Lord *Rama*, "Brother, why do you always want to meet these *Maharishis*, even if you have to go out of your way to do so? Besides meditating all the time, is there anything else they do?" To satisfy *Laxman's* curiosity, Lord *Rama* said, "*Laxman*, it is only the blessed who get an opportunity of meeting such souls. Just the fact of being close to them has a miraculous effect on you. Like the sun, they pass their energy to your mind, body and soul. That energy transports you from darkness to light and from being confined within limits to the limitless." True Masters have much to offer. Every minute spent with them transforms you. Their grace works like insurance and comes handy in times of need.

Call it my good fortune or God's grace that I was able to see such an exalted spirit for which I have only God to thank.

SAI BABA - MY GOD IN HUMAN FORM

There are innumerable legends about *Shirdi Sai Baba's* magical healing powers. People from all over, irrespective of their faith, religion, caste or creed, flocked to him for succour only to go back relieved of their mental or physical problems. Baba invoked the name of Allah, Ram or Bhagwan, different names of the Supreme entity that rules the Universe. To some he is a *Fakir* (*Sufi*) or a holy man, but in reality he is higher than all religions: a saint sent by God to serve humanity. People around and in distant places heard about *Shirdi Sai Baba's* divine qualities and came to pay homage. It is believed that those who met him became his devotees for life. Baba transformed their lives and some of them surrendered themselves totally. They gave up their worldly lives and started living in *Shirdi* as his disciples. Sai Baba equipped them wherewithal to serve the humanity. Learned *Pandits*, who thought he was illiterate discovered that he could not only teach philosophy but also interpret the sacred writings of India more profoundly and clearly than anyone else they had ever known. But he always led his disciples along the Bhakti Marg, the radiant pathway of divine love, self-surrender and devotion.

To love and care for his devotees was the ruling motif of all Baba's actions. Many confirmed that it was in his presence that they felt spiritual exaltation.

They forgot their pains and anxieties. They felt completely safe and the hours passed unnoticed in blissful happiness. It was in 1975 that I along with my family visited this holy place.

They say that *Sathya Sai Baba* is the incarnation of Shirdi Sai Baba. He was born in a village by the name of *Puttaparthi* (Andhra Pradesh) in India on 23rd November, 1926. His mother's name was *Easwaramma* and father's name was *Pedda Raju*. The year 1926 was known as *Akshaya*, meaning the "Never declining, Ever full" year, and 23rd November, according to the old calendar was a day to be devoted to the worship of the God of Gods - *Mahadeva* (Lord Siva). Moreover, in the year 1926 a certain juxtaposition of the stars made the day even more auspicious for Lord Siva's worship. So the villagers were already out chanting the names of Lord Siva when the rising sun outlined the purple rocky hill beyond the yellow sands of *Chitravati* River in *Puttaparthi*. It was exactly the moment when the child *Satyanarayana* entered this world in the cottage of *Pedda Raju*. He was given this name because his mother always invoked the blessings of that particular form and name of God. Actually *Narayana* is another appellation of Vishnu, the second god in the Hindu Trinity, while *Satya* in Sanskrit means 'truth.' *Satyanaranaya* can be interpreted as "true all - pervading God". In India it is not considered odd or profane to name a child in this way. Most Indians, men and women, bear one or more of the thousands of names of God.

Soon after His birth, the baby was placed on some bed sheets spread on the floor. Just then the woman in the room noticed that those sheets were moving up and down in a peculiar way as if there were something alive underneath. To their astonishment it was a Cobra. But the snake did not harm the child.

People present in that room may have thought that the appearance of the cobra was auspicious as cobra is one of the symbols of Lord Siva. People also said that Sai Baba of Shirdi had, on several occasions, appeared before his followers in the form of a cobra.

On the morning of May 23, 1940, that child *Satyanarayana* was only 14 years old when he declared himself as Shirdi Sai Baba. He declared that the time had come to meet his devotees in person. To begin with, people were skeptical, but soon they heard and saw Sai Baba's divine qualities and gathered around him. His devotees came in throngs not only from India but also from the whole world. Even now Baba does not travel outside India. People hear about him and suddenly have an irrepressible urge to go and see him. People believe that it is only when a person gets a call, he/she comes to *Puttaparthi.* They say you can visit Puttaparthi only if Baba wills it.

There are thousands of miracles Sai Baba performs before the public. He uses his miraculous powers to cure their ailments, to help them in their day-to-day problems, to protect them from danger wherever they happened to be and to draw them towards a spiritual way of life. Other types of miracles attributed to him include giving protection to people who are somewhere far away, such as protecting them against accidents, illness and death, blessing the childless with an issue, appearing to people in dreams with advice and help to solve their problems. Many of Baba's more devoted followers have experienced signs of his subtle presence in the form of footprints in ash spread on the floor, a passing vision of his form and other manifestations like that. Strong vibrations are like a ripple in the water, one following this path can feel them.

Like *Jesus*, Baba is able to chase away the evil spirits from those victimized by them and cure the most terrible diseases, such as blindness, palsy and leprosy.

I know there are people who do not believe in miracles. In this context, I quote a Q&A article, which appeared in Times of India on 16th May 2005 by *Sadhguru Jaggi Vasudev*.

"What is this phenomenon we refer to as miracles and healing that cannot be explained by medical science?

Anything you don't understand, you call a miracle. Life happens in many different ways. You have limited yourself to just the physical, the logical – physical in experience, logical in thinking. Anything beyond this, you term as a miracle. That's why I keep reminding you that if there is a miracle, then everything in existence is a miracle, every atom is a miracle, isn't it? Can you believe that a little atom – these three things rotating around each other – if you break it, it becomes an enormous bomb that can destroy the whole planet? Is it not a miracle? Every atom is a miracle. Otherwise, there are no miracles and everything is just the way it is. It is natural. Whether you call it natural or miracle, it's the same thing, just different words. Anything that is not in your perception or part of your experience, you tend to call it a miracle.

There are no miracles in the way you are thinking. The medical science is limited to the knowledge of the physical body. If anything happens beyond that, you think it's a miracle. The life energy in you created your whole body. These bones, this flesh, this heart, the kidneys and everything else. So if a part is damaged, can't it be re-created? If your energies are kept in full flow and proper balance, they are capable of recreating the physical.

My children and I had Baba's *darshan,* actually only saw him for the first time in Delhi in 1973. I had heard so much about his reputation as a great healer. At that time it was almost impossible to see Baba from close quarters because of the large crowds, but we were very lucky to see him from close quarters, sitting and looking at us. Somewhere deep down in some corner of my heart, the deep impression that he left on my psyche was here to stay. After 24 long years, in March 1997 I had a tremendous urge to visit Baba, which I did and became a dedicated devotee of his. Since then I pray to Baba to call me as often as possible to Puttaparthi in Andhra Pradesh and to the 'White Field' in Bangalore. Baba resides in Puttaparthi in a very big Ashram and goes to White Field in Bangalore just for a couple of months during summer time when it is extremely hot in Andhra Pradesh.

Ever since my visit to him in March 1997, I have been very lucky to visit these two places on an average once a year for a month-long stay over there. The aura of the place recharges my spiritual battery and replenishes the energy, which get depleted in between. Just being close to this light gives me tremendous happiness and a feeling of peace and tranquility. Baba's *darshan* (seeing), participation in Bhajan Mandali, joining the group to sing devotional songs, doing *Seva* (service), *Sadhna* (meditation), makes you altogether a different human being. One goes there with lots of doubts and questions in mind but returns with a firm belief and with all the answers.

Baba keeps changing you constantly, knowing how much dose of medicine is to be given to each one of his devotees. This teacher sometime gives you drubbing, deliberately hurts you, crushes your ego and inflicts mental pain on you so that you grow. At the same time, he calls himself a mother, loves and nurses you, feeds you, teaches you, guides you, pats you and comforts you. Seeing is believing, that is all I can say from my own experience. His main aim is truly the spiritual evolution of his devotees.

At the Ashram Baba conveys His views and massages to me through telepathy. Whenever I close my eyes after the *darshan*, His message gets passed on to me with His energy flowing from him to me. If I ask a question, his reply either comes to me in a flash or it takes a lot of time to reach me. During this period of waiting, He instructs me like a teacher to be detached from my involvements at home which are the cause of my anxiety and pain. By the time the answer is given that pain and anxiety have already disappeared. This is the way he answers your questions. He does not want us to be attached to His outward form and says "Learn to live in my spirit. Always help anyone you can, but never hurt anyone." He is the Emperor of the souls.

Baba's services to humanity are difficult to list but some of the well known include:

1. Free hospitals for heart surgery, neuro-surgery and treatment of kidney and various other ailments.

2. Free schools and colleges

3. Distribution of free food for poor children.
4. Pension for widows.
5. Home for the homeless.

This is what little I know about Baba!

Radha Soami, Beas

It all happened at the spur of the moment as if it was preordained. I happened to be in Delhi for a day. Just then my friend *Urvashi* was getting ready to go to Beas, also known as *Dera*.

I had waited for years to visit the *Dera ashram*. Being my first trip, I was reluctant to go there without proper guidance. Thanks to Mrs. *Janak Gorwani*, whom I call aunty, a dedicated *Radha Soami* since she was 13 years old and now secretary of the Radha Soami sect in Rajasthan chalked out the programme for us. Our stay at *Dera* was to be arranged in her magnificent house there. As a part of our programme we were to attend both morning and evening discourses and above all have a personal audience with a true living master of the Dera known as *Babaji*. Master calls and you go, and that is exactly what happened to us. As luck would have it, we were outside the gates of Dera waiting to take a car pass, when the Master crossed us in his car, throwing a glance towards us as though he was welcoming us to Dera.

It is a long drive from *Delhi* to *Beas*. Beas is a river in Punjab where this beautiful small township is situated on its west bank. *Amritsar*, a big city of Punjab, is about forty five minutes drive from this place. The spot was originally chosen by *Jaimal Singh* (1839-1903) and later *Maharaj Sawan Singh*, his successor named the place Dera Baba Jaimal Singh in honour of his Master's memory. A garden town, it has about 500 lush green lawns. The *satsang* halls have the capacity to hold congregations of over 2 lac people at a time. There are many dining halls, snacks bars, and a modern library with a collection of over 5 lacs books. The devotees are humble and flock to the Dera for the love of their Master.

There is a discourse in the morning at Dera everyday. Every Sunday morning there is a discourse by the Master himself. On Saturday and Sunday evening discourses take place in English. Throughout Dera, there is an atmosphere of peace and tranquility.

Maharaj Charan Singh (1916-1990) born in Punjab (Moga), India, a disciple of *Maharaj Sawan Singh* of Beas was widely known as a lawyer by profession. In 1951 Maharaj Jagat Singh made him his successor. He was the head of the Dera for the next four decades. Maharaj ji travelled throughout India and the world giving discourses and initiating seekers, while teaching people to recite the name (the dynamic creative principle, Reality, God) and exhorted people to rise above differences of religion, race and culture. Before his death in 1990, he appointed Baba Gurinder Singh as his successor.

Babaji gave a personal audience to all three of us (myself, Urvashi and her husband Brig. Surjit Singh) at his residence, showing us the way of life for our spiritual evolution. Nothing can give more joy and bliss (not even an Empire) than the proximity to a true Master. One has to be like the proverbial swan, picking up pearls, which lie scattered all around these great Masters. Grateful that I got the opportunity for an audience, it is difficult to write about such souls because it is beyond human capacity to know them with our poorly developed minds.

There is another incident, which is closely related to Babaji giving a personal audience to the three of us. In November 1991, an elderly gentleman named Ronnie Guiney came to my salon from South Africa. He was on his way to Beas. While talking to me he told me his baggage had been misplaced and hadn't arrived when he landed at the Delhi airport. He checked into a hotel and was still waiting to hear from the concerned airline. While sharing he looked rather uncomfortable. On my asking him what in particular was he missing the most, he said it was his electric shaver, something he cannot do without. I had a brand new one lying at home, which I had bought for Dev on one of my trips abroad. Since Dev wasn't using it, I gave it to him the next day. He was grateful and so touched by the gesture of mine that he thanked me profusely and promised to return it on his way back to South Africa.

He was a Radha Swami and visited Dera (Beas) quite often. He too loved his Master. Anyway I forgot about the incident. But after a month, he sent the electric shaver through somebody who left it in my salon. Soon afterwards I received a letter from him from South Africa in which he called me a 'real star'. This was the best compliment any stranger has ever given to me. But his blessing made all the difference to me when Babaji, the master, gave me personal audience at Beas. Good deeds are always rewarded.

In my personal audience with Babaji, I talked to him about this book of mine and told him that I am no celebrity that a publisher would like to publish this book. With a smile on his lips Babaji's answer was short and sweet: "Why not? If the matter in it is good."

GREAT SAYINGS

Let me share with you some of the pearls of wisdom, which I have gathered during my spiritual journey in this world.

◈ All the misfortunes of men derive from one single thing, which is their inability to be at ease in a room (alone).

◈ True religion is the life we lead, not the creed we profess.

◈ You cannot predict to what heights you can soar until you spread your wings.

◈ One goes to the mountain to find oneself, one goes within to find the mountain.

◈ What comes from the heart touches the heart.

◈ The measure of greatness is not the number of servants you have but the number of people you serve.

◈ Charity is twice blessed – it blesses the one who gives and the one who receives.

◈ We make a living by what we get, but we make a life by what we give.

◈ Riches are blessings only to those who make them a blessing to others.

◈ Good intentions die, unless they are executed.

◈ Success in life should be determined by contributions, not accumulations.

◈ Pioneers turn weakness into strength, obstacles into stepping-stones and disaster into triumph.

◈ What I kept, I lost; what I spent, I had; what I

gave, I have.

◈ When things get rough, remember, it's the rubbing that brings out the shine.

◈ Some find life worth living – other make life worth living.

◈ If we take care of our work, the results of our work would take care of us.

◈ Good relationships are hard to find and once developed must be NURTURED.

◈ What you are is God's gift to you but what you make yourself is your gift to God.

◈ It is more important to be human than to be important.

◈ There is no better way to become friends than laughing together.

◈ The earth we abuse and the living things we kill will in the end, take their revenge; in exploiting their presence we are diminishing our future.

◈ Gross things have a tendency to stay; for subtler things, you have to make an effort to retain them.

◈ There is no ideal relationship, no ideal home and no ideal job. It's a fallacy to look for one. The real ideal situation is inside us.

****

4
Count His Blessings

I consider myself blessed to be born in this land of ours and thank my parents for bringing me into this world. I still remember that ever since I was little a girl I often wondered, "Why am I here? What is the purpose of my coming into this world as a human being?" The answer came to me when I heard a saying "Do not take life as problem. It is a mystery to be lived with."

Who you are, where you are born is all a mystery. So is the fact that each one of us is different from the other. Not only the physical features but also the path each one of us treads right to the very end. Singers, dancers, poets, musicians, artists, scientists, designers, and actors are all a part of the society we live in. The saying goes, "God give me serenity to accept what I cannot change and the wisdom to know the difference". Life is a school from which we never graduate. Make this your guiding principle and the search ends. After this, there is nothing more to know.

I was hardly four years old when I nearly drowned in a tank in our village. I had gone there with our domestic help whose family had served us for generations. All the children were very fond of him and he too loved us. *Ramdhan Dada*, that's what we called him, was much younger to my father. When I requested him to sit outside and wait for me, he refused, but when I insisted he let me go down the steps of the tank alone. As I sat down on the last step and touched the water, I slipped and fell headlong into the water. By the time he realized that I was drowning, I was already drifting away from the steps towards deep water. He immediately jumped into the tank and pulled me out. He held me upside down to let the water flow out from my stomach. I was breathless. The water had entered my eyes, nose and ears. At that age, I did not know how to swim. That accident gave me inspiration to learn swimming.

******

I was so impressed by a beauty salon where I used to go for my haircut, as a teenager, in Poona that I started nourishing a strong desire to own one like that when I grew up. Little did I know that years later this was going to be my profession for twenty-two long years of my life. I ran one of the most successful beauty salons in one of the most beautiful places in India, known as *Rambagh Palace* in *Jaipur*, a prestigious place known for its beautiful gardens and an enchanting environment.

******

I had a strong wish to become a horse-rider especially after reading (schoolgirls) comics at a very young age. This wish of mine was fulfilled later when I became a good horsewomen and got some prizes at the national level. I continued horse riding till my children grew up.

******

Having seen many beautiful houses, I too wanted to have a luxurious, beautiful house of my own. My Creator blessed me not with one but two houses. When things have to go your way, you meet the right person at the right time, and that's what happened to me. By chance when I went to see my friend in Delhi I was really impressed by the design of her mother-in-law's house. She gave me the address and telephone number of the architect. The land was purchased and a house of my dreams was ultimately constructed. I often wonder if our inner power is so great that wishes can come true. Yes, you have to experience it to know it. They say that God helps those who help themselves.

******

United States of America is undoubtedly one of the most fascinating countries. The more one knows about its great people, its fabulous wealth and its geography as well as its unique democratic traditions, the more one wants to go and see it with one's own eyes. I too had always cherished the desire to visit the country, but as they say, there is a time for everything and there is some power, which determines when you are going to tread any land.

It came to me as a golden opportunity when my daughter and son-in-law went to *USA* for a long stay in *Michigan* where the latter had gone to do his masters in hospital administration. During their stay I visited USA three times and making Michigan my base I stayed with my children for six months and travelled extensively from north to south and saw almost every place worth seeing.

******

While looking after my business, I came in touch with people from different parts of the world. Whenever anyone talked of *India,* I used to tell them, "If you really want to see whole of India you have to make at least three trips because it is such a vast country with its different areas having different cultures, climates and geographical features. All its states are different from one another." I never realized that those words of mine were applicable to me as well. Later when I started visiting foreign lands I realized that going to a country once was not enough. You have to go there several times to know the land and understand the people of that country. I was fortunate to see most of the countries three or four times. Very often people do not follow the advice that they give to others.

******

A day before I finished my twentieth year in business, I received a call from a girl from *'Times of India'* asking me if I could spare some time for an interview which would be published in that newspaper. Preoccupied, I told her to call in the following week. However, when she called again and requested to conduct the interview on the phone, I readily agreed. She asked me a number of questions and in about half an hour it was over though I could not figure out why she was reluctant to give me her name.

The text of the interview appeared in the papers after a couple of days. Everything about my work and myself was written so well in such a short time that I decided to call her up at her office, but she was not there. No one had any idea of her whereabouts. This was probably the direct reward for me from God.

I reproduce here exactly what she wrote: "There is a cosy place at Rambagh Palace Hotel where you may go if you are feeling miserable about those blackheads or an unwanted sun tan and come out, rejuvenated and beautiful. It is a legacy in the making. Asha Ranawat's parlour has now been there for twenty years. A skilful rider and swimmer, Ranawat is also heavily into travelling. We got her to talk about the finer points behind her success.

Her comments were as follows:

1. Keep your mental faculties open and follow your instinct. Spirituality and practicality go hand in hand.

2. Be systematic in your approach. Once you decide on your goal, show motivated efforts in its direction.

3. If you inflict pain on your peers to climb the ladder of success in the fastest way, you also get hurt in the hardest way.

4. Show due respect towards others. Do not take undue advantage of your position.

5. Charity, along with your work, yields satisfaction like nothing else.

6. Be very independent and develop your inner strength. If you are righteous, your soul will pull you through any hurdles that may come your way.

7. Work with wholehearted dedication. Channelise all your energy for constructive work.

8. Commitment and hard work have no substitutes. There is absolutely no short cut to hard work.

9. Pray every day and meditate to keep yourself going.

10. Finally, people do not really change; so do not try to change them. People do get on your nerves, but the show must go on. When someone's being

nasty just plug in your ears or laugh it off.

11. One can pull on only with love and humility.

12. Believe in giving but do not expect, this is the key to happiness that no one can rob of you.

******

My intuitive power has always been very good. It became stronger with meditation. When I see a person, I can tell what sort of person he is, despite attempts to conceal the real self. I take it that intuitive power is a divine gift to me. My aunts and friends have often told me that whenever I came in their thoughts or was being remembered by them, I got in touch with them either through a phone call or personally.

******

At times when I have missed a flight or a train, I felt that Providence was taking care of me in its own way. It was a way of communicating to me that time was neither ripe nor right to travel. Such things can only be experienced when one sits back and lets Destiny take over the invisible Hand which has worked out the minutest detail for mortals to mutely follow.

******

In 1984, when I felt a keen desire to learn about various religions, Mrs. *Mumtaz Baqar* entered my life miraculously. She was an elderly, well-qualified lady who had retired from the WHO. She was a true Muslim. No more in this world, she had shared her life's experiences with me - an ocean of wisdom. Now I remember her, cherishing her advice and replaying the lessons which life had taught her.

Mumtaz lost her husband when she was very

young. With two children to bring up, there was little support from her own parents. Her older sister found favour from her mother who was always indifferent towards Mumtaz. Later Mumtaz lost her daughter in an air crash at a tender age, who was an airhostess in the Indian Air Lines. Mumtaz braved this also but whenever she spoke of her she could not help breaking down.

To me Mumtaz was aunty Baqar: one because there was a considerable age difference and the other because I respected her. From her I learnt the basics of Islam. I visited her twice in Chennai where she had settled down. She also gave me a poster with a picture of a small cottage underneath which was inscribed: "To a friend's house the road is never too long." To date that poster is placed near my dressing table reminding me of her along with the cruel fact that she is no more.

******

Another lady, *Geeta Nath*, the wife of an army doctor told me about *Christianity* and the teachings in the *Bible*. Born a *Hindu*, *Geeta* converted to Christianity (*Penticostal*) out of choice. I accompanied her to the church on several occasions and also met some pastors. Strangely my own house in the army area was next to a church. The vibrations that I felt the message seeping within me. It was *Geeta* who offered prayers before my present house was constructed. I recall her words: "Lord, grant this place a beautiful house," and it certainly is a beautiful house. We have not met each other for years now but I do thank her always and think of her with love and affection. Should we not call this a blessing?

Another person, *Salma Moosa*, who became a

good friend of mine from South Africa to Jaipur to do business, became a good friend. She gave me a *Tasbi* (a rosary). It is because of her that I made it a point to visit beautiful mosques in *Kualalumpur* and *Faisil Masjid* in Islamabad on my next trip and the *Dargah Sharif* in Ajmer several times when my son was studying in Mayo College.

****

5
Some Images of Divine Help

During childhood, I loved butterflies. My best moments were to see them flutter around the garden, trying my best to catch them or at best feel the soft texture of their wings and observe the layers of different hues. Often I would put them in a jar and observe their movements. Later in my life, a black butterfly with white dots on its wings became a symbol of spiritual power or light for me. Its appearance was auspicious because whenever I was in difficulty it gave an indication that things were moving in the positive direction. It would appear from nowhere, often at an odd hour before dawn, and rest somewhere close to me. I would get solace in my difficult and trying times a clear indication that a Power was protecting me.

I recall an incident in *Munich* (*Germany*), in 1981 where I had gone to attend a cosmetic fare. Cosmetologists from all over the world had gathered there to display their latest cosmetics, beauty equipments and machines. Pretty girls from different companies showed their skills and expertise by using their latest make-up techniques on anyone who wanted to have the experience. They tried their hand on me and a complete video film was made on how they did it. Gosh! How different I looked? But that unforgettable incident happened while I was making purchases at the fare. Having purchased something I picked up a packet but left my wallet at the cash counter, which had all my cash and travellers' cheques. After almost half an hour, somebody tapped me on my back. As I turned back I saw a lady with glasses standing right in front of me looking at me furiously. She had my wallet in her hand and the moment I faced her she started admonishing me in *German*. All I could make out was that she was behind me in the queue at the cash counter where I made the payment. She probably decided to trace me and return the wallet. There being a huge crowd in the fare I simply wonder how she traced me. Her honesty simply made me bow my head with respect for the people of *Deutch Land*. I hugged her, kissed her and thanked her zillion times. I can never forget that face and those beautiful eyes behind the glasses. I was really grateful to her, imagine a person without any money in the foreign land! It was a miracle. Once again I knew it was my God and once again I thanked Him.

******

In July, 1981, *Jaipur* was inundated: a desert land where rains lashed. My entire household baggage was lying in the basement of my parents farm house. At that time Dev was posted to a non-family station, *Sikkim* (Yakhla pass), at the height of 17000 feet. Children were away in their boarding schools and I had just returned from *Europe*. The whole house was covered with water. A housewife collects things all her life to decorate her house. I was no exception. But for the recent shopping in *Europe*, everything I had was under water. My mother and father were even more worried than me. They had seen my collection of curios, carpets and furniture, but I took it in my stride. Once the water was drained out of the basement, everything was put to dry. It took quite sometime drying up every single thing and getting everything back into shape. However, God was on my side and the losses were not much. During this time *Dr. Bhatia* and his wife, *Dr. Meena*, who are very good friends of ours had come to stay with us from *Ferozepur*, after closing their full time nursing home for a couple of days.

As usual this too was a surprise visit from them. They could always smell trouble and always land up as my saviours at a time of a crisis. Thanks to them that we sorted out everything more easily and earlier than expected. Once again my God came to my rescue. They have two pretty daughters *Deepa* and *Rupa*.

******

In summer of 1991 while visiting my daughter in *Michigan*, I had great urge to see my master in *Malibu* (*Los Angles*) where he resided. It was with great difficulty that I got permission from *Mahatma Sampurnanand*, a very old devotee of the Master, who had been with him since his childhood days. He told me quite frankly that chances were, I may not be able to see the Master because most of the time he was traveling and even when he was in town, he was very busy. But in my hearts of heart, I knew that my Master would be there. A friend of mine in Miami had guided me on how to reach there. I drew a rough map along with the names of places. But when I reached there something unusual happened. I passed that spot and went further ahead missing his place. I got dropped at a wrong place. It was my fault entirely. Now there was no other way except to walk to the nearest bus stop which was at quite a distance from there. In those days that was the only transport available. According to the information, a bus arrived there after every one hour. My problem was that a friend of mine had already arranged a car to pick up at the foot of hill and drive me up to the Master's residence at 11.00 a.m. Being a private place not everybody was allowed to go up and also since it was located at quite a distance from there, it was hard to reach there. I prayed to the Master and an idea struck to my mind - why not ask for a lift? All of a sudden I noticed a big car coming my way from a distance with two or three people sitting in it. I moved my hand up, it came to a screeching halt. I ran towards it and pulling out the piece of paper with a drawing made by me and explained the whole thing to the gentleman who was driving. The gentleman looked worried and told me that I had come far ahead leaving the place far behind and that he had to drive ahead. But suddenly he looked at me and said, "Never mind, I'd drive you back, as we are not in a hurry." Not in a hurry in the United States of America sounded very surprising! As I got into his car, I introduced myself to him, his wife and two adorable kids, one of them was barely few months old. I had no words to thank him for this kind gesture of his. We talked very little, I knew all along, it was all due to that divine energy which my Master had taught me to get in touch with. It was quite a drive back. The car, which was waiting for me, was about to turn back when I reached there. I shouted from where I was and asked the car to stop. The timing was perfect! I was so moved that I did not know how to thank this family. I hugged each one of them and my tears started rolling down my eyes. They hardly knew who I was and yet they went out of their way to help me. It was again a stranger who appeared from nowhere to help me. I feel sorry that I missed asking them their names, but their faces remain ever fresh in my mind. Even today, I bless them from the core of my heart.

While being driven up the hill by this lady to the Master's residence, my heartbeat kept getting faster. But within my heart I knew that my Master would be there. As we got down from the car, I saw him coming down the steps of his garden in casual clothes. There were some other people who too had come there to see him. Later he came outside to be with us.

Master surely had chosen one of the most beautiful spots on the earth to make his house. The front of the house overlooked the vast blue sea. Located at a great height on a hill there was nothing in between the house and sea. The other three sides overlooked the green and thick jungles. What a peaceful and serene place it was! Master often said to us in his discourses, "Find a beautiful, heavenly place for yourself to live. If there is heaven anywhere, it is on this earth."

******

A programme was scheduled in *Delhi* Ashram of the Master. This time my son Rohit was also with me. The Ashram being big and spread out on a large piece of land was located at a fairly long distance from *Delhi*. Taxi drivers usually don't want to go there because while coming back, they don't get passengers. However, we hired a taxi and as usual the driver kept complaining all the way. As we were in a hurry to reach there and did not want to miss out on the discourse, we got fed up and asked him to stop. We got down from his taxi, paid him and told him to go back. As my son and I thought that we were stuck and tried to find a way out, a white coloured chauffer-driven Mercedes Benz stopped near us. For a moment I was in two minds - whether to get into it or not - when all of a sudden a thought came flashing that this was arranged for us in this special way because master wanted us to be there. We didn't say a word to the driver, but he dropped us where our destination was. We thanked the driver. We were just in time for the discourse.

A programme of this nature scheduled by the Master is always a special occasion in my life. There are times when one feels, life is at a standstill. At a time like that one does not want to do anything. But for me life is an exciting adventure, thrilling and mysterious because attending such programmes is spiritually uplifting experience for me. I would hate it to be otherwise. On one such occasion, there came a call from Ashram for me to participate in planting some flower trees. We call it *service* or *seva.* Working together with people from different parts of the world for fifteen days was not only a matter of great joy for me but also a lesson in cultivating humility and compassion for all forms of life.

******

In the beginning of April 1996, another programme was scheduled for the people of *Rajasthan, Gujarat* and *Delhi,* which was to take place in two parts. I was scheduled to leave for Poona after the first segment. My air ticket had been bought a while ago.

Leaving the Master was always a sad moment and as I sat down in the taxi, tears started rolling down my eyes. I felt dead and lifeless. On reaching the airport, I straightaway headed for the counter and handed over my ticket. To my surprise, the lady at the counter gave the ticket back to me saying that I was booked for a month later: "The ticket" she told me was for May 5 and not April!" I couldn't believe it. Such a thing had never happened to me before because being a frequent traveller I always checked the tickets carefully. I quickly came back, feeling happy and to my surprise I was given the same accommodation where I was staying before. It seemed that some superior power had brought me back to experience some of the happiest days of my life. As the *Holi* festival fell from the 6th to 8th April, it was celebrated amidst great fun and revelry. On top of it when I reached home, I got the happy news from my daughter that I was going to be a grandmother!

******

Once I got an opportunity to touch Sai Baba's feet, but soon after I experienced acute pain in my lower abdomen. It was so acute that I started sweating profusely with pain. For a moment I thought maybe I have done something wrong! This pain was choking me. Is Baba angry with me? And all of a sudden it stopped. It was then that I remembered I had been advised by a gynaecologist to undergo surgery as soon as possible. After the incident, when I went back to the doctor, he told me that now there was no need for any operation. Now I can't help thinking that it was a case of a quick surgery performed by Baba's healing touch.

******

On one of my visits to Baba in July 2003, I slipped from top of the staircase and came down six to eight steps landing on the floor with a thud. It had just stopped raining and there was water all over. In fact I was in a hurry to be in time for the evening *bhajans*. After the fall, I said to myself, "This is the end of my stay, as I probably have a terrible fracture." *Janica*, a friend of mine, tried helping me get up which seemed next to impossible due to immense pain in my left foot. But by the grace of God, after placing some ice cubes on my foot for a while, I was able to walk and though limping, reached the hall and listened to bewitching *bhajan* of Baba. The swelling and pain lasted for some days but I was able to walk. Having received good medical attention at Baba's hospital, I was soon all right. It was only a sprained ankle and the recovery was quick. But I must say but for the timely help given to me by my friend Janica, it could have taken much longer to heal.

******

Once while visiting *Baba* I met a young boy who was hardly seventeen. How he was chosen by Baba to heal others in *U.K.* was a story by itself. His parents and grandfather were ardent devotees of Baba and had a beautiful temple in their house with a big altar dedicated to Baba. This boy was only fourteen when his grandfather, who was a diabetic, died of gangrene, even after his leg was amputated. Even when he was alive his pain was so acute that no amount of medication would give him any relief. This boy loved his grandfather and was deeply attached with him. On top of it, his own father was an invalid and moved around in a wheelchair. All their prayers to Baba were of no avail. His faith in Baba was never as deep as that of his sister. After his grandfather's death, he became a drug addict and started smoking, drinking and eating non-vegetarian food despite the fact that everyone in his family was a vegetarian. Somewhat a rebel, there was no way anyone could manage him. His parents were heartbroken but their faith in Baba remained as firm as ever.

Once, they succeeded in bringing him to Baba in *Puttaparthi.* Next day during the morning *darshan*, Baba saw him and asked the boy to come and meet him in the interview room soon after *darshan.* At

Baba's place when anyone was asked to meet, people accompanying him/her all went together. In this case too his mother got up from the ladies section and father of course from the men's section, where he was sitting, in the wheelchair. They were standing in the *varandah* which is just outside the interview room when Baba asked his father to go back. The mother and the boy were then taken in, which totally put the boy off more so because his father was a patient and needed Baba's help more than him. Baba looked into the eyes of the boy, smiled and said, "Oh! Blue eyes, beautiful." Actually he was wearing blue-coloured contact lenses. The boy said nothing. Baba materialized *Vibhuti*, which is sacred ash and gave it in boy's hand and asked him to eat all of it and leave nothing behind. The boy did that and then was asked to leave along with his mother. They all flew back to *U.K.* This boy became from bad to worse. Under the influence of alcohol, he nearly gave up school and relentlessly pursued the path of self-destruction. Then suddenly when he was very sick, he asked a friend if he had a picture of *Sai Baba*. His friend, who was clueless, replied in the negative. Meanwhile this boy's condition worsened and he thought he was going to die. But he came back home because he had a great urge to see Baba. As he came near the temple and saw Baba's alter, he vomited. He could not believe, the vomit consisted only of *Vibhuti*. He vomited again. Now the *vibhuti* started coming out of his ears, hands, nose, hair & eyes. He was drenched with *vibhuti*, right from head to toe. He was terribly scared and wanted to shout and cry. Suddenly, he felt that Baba had stepped out of the altar as Lord *Narayan*. A *chakra* was moving round His head and a light glowed from his palm. There was smile on his lips and both hands of his were raised in a gesture of blessing him. The boy was shocked. Yes! He is a God as his parents told him. Slowly Baba moved backwards and disappeared. This was a turning point in his life. Next day onwards, he started praying and did what his parents asked him to do. He sang *bhajans* with his family. He also acquired a *japmala* (string of beads) which one uses while praying. Now he wanted to go to Baba on his own. Consequently he came again with his family to India. The following day, at the time of morning *darshan,* Baba saw him with *japmala* in his hand and remarked, "Óh, a *japmala*?" Baba again asked him to see him alone after the *darshan* in the interview room. When he went there as he was asked to do, Baba didn't say anything about his past. Instead he said," Son, I want you to reach out to people who have problems like you and also who are sick with various diseases. Baba materialized a silver ring, which He made him wear on his right hand ring finger, which fitted him perfectly. Then he materialized an engraved silver box with a lid (the size of a match box) and showed him how to fill his box with *vibhuti.* He was to hold the box in his left hand and then keep tapping it with the ring until it got filled up. The boy did that and on opening the lid found that the box was full of vibhuti. Baba asked him to give this *vibhuti* to needy people and instructed him never to let it become empty. Always see to it that there is some *Vibhuti* left, before fresh *vibhuti* is materialised again.

Ever since, the young boy has been doing a lot of work serving the sick as instructed by Baba and has also become a great devotional singer. Many of us had the good luck to listen and see the boy who had undergone this beautiful experience. The boy showed us everything during a *bhajan* session in the hall in one of the devotee's place residing permanently in Puttaparthi. All of us who were present there were given little Vibhuti from that very small box. After coming back to Jaipur, I shared this experience with all the devotees of Baba who gather on every Thursday for an evening session of *bhajan* singing, and as I did that, a beautiful rose dropped from Baba's altar.

Another unique experience that I had on one of my visits was about a young girl who was hardly twenty. That girl was suffering from cancer and looked so frail, so lifeless and weak. She had come there with her mother and was sitting in front of me for the morning *darshan*. She had lost her hair, may be because of the medical treatment she was undergoing. Baba called her for an interview. She was given Vibhuti in the form of tablets materialized by Baba and was asked to consume them. She told us later that they were bitter. After that when I saw her, I was surprised. She was smiling, walking as though nothing had ever been wrong with her health. Baba had asked her to stay back for some more time, maybe because she needed treatment. Normally, it was very difficult to trace people at the ashram, but when Baba wanted us to witness certain things, the person came along and either sat down close to us or was introduced to us by Baba so that we knew what was happening.

Baba always attended to the needy person during the morning *darshan* in no time by asking that person for an interview. In a crowd of thousands of people He knew who needed Him the most.

******

I will always remember 25th October, 1990, as

it also happens to be my son's birthday. Just before going to sleep, I prayed and thanked my soul for giving me such a wonderful day and for also taking such good care of my son all these years. As I was about to go to my bed, on an impulse I placed my hand on my right breast. Suddenly I felt it had a little lump on it. As I pressed it, some liquid started oozing out of it. Since the lights had been switched off, I had no idea about what it could be. I hurried to the bathroom and switched on the lights. My hand was red with blood and my nightclothes too were smeared by it. I immediately realized that I had a serious problem, which needed to be addressed urgently. Going back to my bed, I picked up my phone and dialled the number of a very good friend of mine, *Dr. Meena Bhatia* at *Ferozepur*, whom I had complete faith in as a doctor. She had been a close friend of mine for the last three decades. She advised me not to take it lightly and visit a surgeon and get mammography done straightaway. The surgeon I went to advised me to go to Delhi and meet another surgeon who specialized in mammography. Following his advice, I went to Delhi and had a thorough check-up done after which, I was asked to wait for two days to see what the report indicated. As soon as the report arrived I was advised to undergo a surgery as soon as possible. I had to get that tiny lump removed. The surgeon who operated upon me did a wonderful job. He did the operation so beautifully leaving absolutely no mark. He too asked me to wait till the report of the biopsy came from *Bombay*. To my surprise, at that very time a conference was to take place in my town and the same doctor was to come from Bombay to attend it. Luckily I was saved the anxiety of waiting. This report too was clear. All along I had faith in my inner light that whatever was happening was for my good. If my time to go had come then I must go and if not then I must keep enjoying this beautiful gift called life.

******

My twenty-two years in business were about to come to an end when I suddenly started thinking whether I should continue with my work or not. With constant driving, I had developed acute pain in my shoulders. My house was far away from the workplace. One day while I was meditating, I posed this question to my inner voice and sought its answer. The answer came: "You are like a caged bird. No one knows your pains. You just open the door of your cage and fly away. Be free and enjoy your freedom." The message conveyed to me was to shut down my business. There was no looking back. Two years have passed since then. These two years have been the most wonderful years of my life. People say when you don't work, you cannot spend. Believe me in these two years, I have spent more money than I have spent in the rest of my life. I bought whatever I liked; travelled to the places which I had missed out seeing earlier and lived in royal manner. Thank God that I listened to my inner voice. Freedom is given to us when we surrender our will to our soul, which is the voice of god. Once you do that, it takes complete charge of your well-being.

******

Recently, I bought a new car. As I entered my house; a black butterfly with white dots came flying down and sat on it twice as though it was inspecting it, and then flew off. This was a clear indication of divine approval and blessings. Nobody believes me when I say that my new car gives me an average fuel consumption of 15 kilometers to a litre. The dealer himself told me its consumption of fuel is not more than 10 km a litre, that too on the higher side! On my second servicing of the car, the workshop manager asked me if I was happy with running of the car and the fuel consumption. I said, "Of course, it's a great car and gives me an average of 15 km. to a litre". He could not believe it. Don't you think it is a miracle? I asked him and he agreed. I laughed loudly and told him, I am used to it, because miracles often happen to me.

******

While driving from *Jaipur* to *Delhi* on 16th April 2005, my car was bashed up from behind on the National Highway. I was at the wheel, while my driver who was sitting on the back seat was hurt. I was slowing down while saving myself from a tractor-trolley which suddenly came on the highway from the left side from a village when a Tata Sumo (taxi) banged into our car from behind. The accident could have been fatal. Both, the driver and I, could have died. It was one of those days when I distinctly felt the divine grace being showered on me.

There is a beautiful temple of *Shirdi Sai Baba* outside *Jaipur*, near *Kukas*, on the way to Delhi. Whenever we pass by, we stop and pray there. This has always been my favourite temple as the statue of Baba installed there is so alive that I literally talk to Him and receive quick answers. On this particular day too, like on many of our previous trips to Delhi I stopped and went in. Early in the morning, Baba's statue was being bathed and the whole place around was being cleaned. I had never seen this sort of cleaning being done before. This day also being my birthday, I wanted Baba to shower extra blessings on me. But what followed came to me as a revelation. As we were driving, we saw a white coloured mini truck with big pictures of Shirdi Sai Baba and Lord Jesus painted on both sides of truck with about six to eight orange-coloured flags flying over it. This truck overtook us and went ahead in the same direction as us. After sometime another similar truck came from behind and went ahead of us. Every time a truck crossed, I prayed and waved to the truck. When a similar truck crossed us the third time, after almost an hour, I told the driver that something very nice was going to happen to us because Shirdi Baba was coming with us right from the temple. I waved and thanked Him and within seconds this taxi hit us from the back. By the time I got down, came the fourth truck and I knew Baba was coming with us to save my life. My life was in danger and He knew it. After the fourth truck, there was no sign of any further danger and we some how reached Delhi.

I am a little ashamed of myself for not thanking Him fully after the accident because I was more concerned about the damage done to the car. Whenever this scene crosses my mind, I pray and seek his forgiveness.

******

In February 1973, after winning the first prize at the Delhi horse show, I went to the stables to kiss my horse. Used to their masters carrying carrots for them. Since mine was a quick trip to the stables, I didn't have anything in my hand except something for the *syais*. When I kissed the forehead of the horse, he bit me playfully on my lip, that I lost part of my lower lip. Had it not been for the miracles in plastic surgery, it would never have been restored to perfection.

******

The wedding of my daughter, which I wanted to be a lavish and a grand one, took lot of my time in planning, shopping and detailing. Being the first wedding in my house, I had little experience. But things worked out and I concluded that hard work and my prayers had paid off.

******

The art of writing for me was making the impossible becoming possible. Inspiration to do so came from within. I remember, after my marriage, my father always complained that why I don't write a letter to him regularly. He once joked that whenever he received a letter from me after a gap of months it was time to call the Pundit (a priest) to find out an auspicious time to read it. I was so touched by his remark that I decided to write to him regularly after that.

If I've learned anything from my experience in this life, it is to have faith in God. God is with us if we falter; He is with us, when we break down and helps us to recover. My life's experience is my biggest wealth. Every experience has given me an inspiration to be a better human being. When I started working in 1981, my family and my parents opposed it because no woman had ever done so in our family. But feeling that I had some responsibility towards my family and myself I broke the tradition and decided to work. I must say I had Dev's support.

****

6
My Travels Abroad

Travelling has always been a passion with me: a desire which was amply fulfilled. People often complain that not knowing the language of a place is a big hurdle in enjoying one's visit abroad. But my travels have convinced me that communicating with people anywhere in the world is hardly a problem. Wherever one goes, one finds that people are as eager to befriend you as much as you are. The language of the heart is understood no matter where you are.

The more I saw God's creation, the more wonderstruck I was with its natural beauty as well as creativity of man all through the ages. Wherever you go, apart from beholding the natural beauty bestowed on a place by its geography, you also see monuments created by human ingenuity which never cease to evoke the admiration of an onlooker.

At this juncture, it is necessary to recount my experiences during my travels to *Europe*, *U.S.A.*, *Japan* and *South-East Asia*.

I was still very young when I started dreaming of visiting *Paris*. I often visualized myself getting off an aircraft and heading towards the city which had captured the imagination of people all over the world for various reasons.

Ironically my first visit abroad was to Paris. Among the places which were topmost on my list were the magestic Arch De Troimphe, the Opera House, Notre Dame Cathedral, Euro Disney, Eiffel Tower, Les invalids, Concorde Square, Place Igor

Starvinsky (the fountain), Champs Elysees, Moulin Rouge with its most beautiful and fashionable women. What really fascinated me were the open air restaurants there, decorated with beautiful flowers like geraniums and petunias, lovely shades and colours of linen with floral designs enhancing the beauty of those restaurants. The espresso coffee there was delicious but one had to acquire a taste for it because of its very strong flavour.

Among the other places that I visited in *France* was *Nice*, known as the capital of Rivera, a fashionable city where people went to relax and have fun. The city had a number of museums and its famous flower market. Relaxing on the beach amidst the blue waters of the *Mediterranean Sea* is nothing short of a wondrous dream. While driving through, we visited Blue grass perfumery where we also saw a demonstration of perfume making.

Monaco and Monte Carlo are one of the smallest states of *Europe* but very highly rated on the tourists' map of *Europe*. The spectacular view of the Mediterranean Sea from *Monte Carlo* is amazing. A visit to the Grand Casino is a special attraction for people who liked gambling, where I too tried my luck at the slot machines. The rich and famous people flock to the casino in their Rolls, Mercedeses, Feraris and B.M.Ws.

NETHERLANDS

On my second and third visit to *Netherlands*, in the year 1999 and 2000, when I was accompanied by my husband, Dev, we decided that instead of going to big cities like *Rottradam* and *Hague* again, we should visit smaller towns and villages, which represent the real beauty and culture of any country. Consequently we went and stayed in a hotel named *De Plasmolen* located in the province of North Brabant, which we thought to be one of the most beautiful spots in the whole area. Located on the banks of a small lake, this hotel was surrounded by a forest with horse-riding tracks going into its interior. The place left a lasting impression on my mind. Later on my return to India, we were shocked to find out that *De Plasmolen* Hotel got burnt down due to a short circuit. Another tragic news that we received later was that a German friend of ours, whose beautiful house located near *De Plasmolen* Hotel we stayed in, was no more. The sweet memories of that lovely person and her lovely house remain in our hearts. We came to know later that her house too was sold away to someone. These incidents made me realize the importance of everything around us - they convinced me that it was always better to enjoy whatever was given to us to its fullest, because the next moment it may not be there. *Boxmeer* was another town, which we visited. It had some of the loveliest houses, gardens and parks; also a tiny shopping area, a beautiful countryside with Dutch restaurants strewn all over. *Arcen*, another small town which we visited because of its famous public park, *Nigmegan*, which was bigger and beautiful and *Klive*, a small border town in *Germany* adjoining *Netherlands*, which had many boutiques worth visiting.

In *Amsterdam*, the world's biggest flower auction is held in *Aalsmeer*, in a complex of the size of hundred football fields put together. Both tulips and asparagus is widely cultivated in *Holland*. The *Keukenof*, the world's largest spring garden with its colourful flower beds that lay amongst ancient trees, stole my heart.

Volendem A little distance from *Amsterdam* lies the picturesque town of Volendem, known for graceful traditional costumes worn by its inhabitants. Its little wooden houses, cheese farms and the wooden shoe factory should not to be missed by anyone visiting *Holland.*

Amsterdam, the Dutch capital is famous for its hundred bridges, old houses along the canal, glass-topped boats for canal cruise across all those bridges, the red light district, National Monument, a 22 meter high Obelisk dedicated to those who died in the World War II. The Molen van Stolen Mill is the only working windmill. Hundreds of exceptionally tall men and women, cycling around the city is a common sight. About 10,000 km. of cycling track has been laid out all over the country. Each province publishes cycling maps. All the main roads have separate bike lanes.

BELGIUM

Bruges in *Belgium,* one of the Europe's best preserved medieval cities is one of the most visited places in the country. *Bruges* (*Brugg* in Flemish) was once a prosperous cloth manufacturing town and a centre for Flemish Primitive Art. This city was located on the banks of Hezuin River. Later when the river got silted, people fled leaving behind deserted canals and homes.

Its richly ornate 13th century business centers remained deserted for five centuries (and have remained the same because of strict building regulation) due to massive slitting of the *Hezuin* River. Walking tours and cruising canals are a few things that are a must for every visitor. From the market rises 83 meter high belfry with its 47 belts Crillon, is home of the Holy blood where a few coagulated drops of Christ's blood are said to be stored.

Brussels, the capital of *Belgium*, is headquarter of *EU* and *NATO* and home to Europe's most impressive Central Square. The renowned grand place and legendary Mannekin Pis Statue, the famous statue of a small weeping boy, St. Michaels Church and the St. Herbert Galleries, Europe's oldest glass covered shopping arcade, the *Belgium* Comic Strip Centre and the Atonium which is a unique structure made of steel are the major attractions of this city.

SWITZERLAND

Switzerland is truly God's own country. I stayed in **Geneva** for sometime and was mesmerized by its natural beauty and vineyards. Situated on the banks of the largest lake Rhone in central *Europe,* people in large numbers flock for recreation and relaxation. Thanks to its 130 Hotels with 14000 beds, it can accommodate a large number of visitors from all over the world.

Today *Geneva* houses some 200 international government and non-governmental organizations including the office of the *United Nations*, to which 150 diplomatic missions are accredited. It is known as the "city of peace".

Geneva is located in the heart of *Europe*. You can visit *France, Germany* or *Italy* in less than half an hour. One can have a beautiful view of this city from the top of *Salve* mountain in *France*. While staying in *Geneva* you can visit nearby towns in *France* like *Divonne*, a place famous for its Thermal Power Centre located at the foot of *Jura* mountain, or go to *Yvore*, famous for its geraniums and Petunia flowers and old souvenir shops. *Evion* is famous for its bottled water. You can also take a trip along the lake by cruise to the Olympic capital, *Lausanne*, go further on a *Montreux* to visit Chillon Castles, one of the *Switzerland's* most beautiful sites that became famous thanks to Lord Byron, who was held a captive here. *Gruyeres*, the magnificent medieval town, which has lent its name to the famous Cheese, was worth a visit too. We took Ronilla & her sons from *Gruyeres* to the chocolate city by a special train for children known as the chocolate train. They had chocolates to their hearts content.

Undertaking a day's excursion, you can visit the village of *Zermatt*, dominated by *Matterhorn*, which is one of the best ways to see the heart of Alpine Switzerland. There one can savour variety of wines. *Fondu, Racllet*, and *Rosti* served throughout *Switzerland*.

While touring *Switzerland, Interlaken*, a valley town not far away from the mighty peaks of *Jungfrau* is a wonderful place to explore the surrounding delights. One such delight is *St. Bernard*, famous for St. Bernard's dogs. It is at a great height and snows in summer as well. You can pick a pup from here. *Lucerne*, another delight is on *German* side of *Switzerland* and is a *German* speaking area, famous for its natural beauty. *Lucarno* offers a heaven for those who want to rest and relax around the lake in summer. Location wise it is Switzerland's lowest town. In the same way *Lugano*, which is southernmost town of *Switzerland* offers an excellent opportunity for holiday makers. It is an excellent place for water sports and hikes to some beautiful sites on the hills.

GERMANY

A documentary film on the Berlin Wall, which divided the German people and separated friends and relatives from one other, that I had seen as a child, remained stuck in my mind for many long years. I got the opportunity to see *Berlin* in June 2001 and stayed with my friend Christine wodestky who was a German flim actress, though the wall had been brought down by then. Inspite of heavy bombing in the World War II, this city has more bridges than *Venice* and more trees than *Paris*.

The Spree River flows across the *Berlin* city. T.V. Tower, Unter den Linden, a fashionable avenue of Old Berlin which includes Karl-Liebkneeth Satrasee, running towards east from Brandenburger to Alexanderplatz. Some of the finest museums are located in this area. The area, which was occupied by the *Berlin* Wall has now become the largest construction site in Europe. American Business Centre has now come up near the old Check Post Charlie. Postsdamer Platz there has become an International Corporation Centre. Postdam, situated on the Hevel River, became an important place in the 17th century as the residence of the Elector of Brandenburg, the royal seat and garrison town. In 18th century, the wealthy gentry made marvelous palaces over here. Fortunately, in 1945 after the British bombed the historic Postdam, all these places remained undamaged. The only Palace, which was hit badly, was the city Palace. Kulturhaus, an old town hall, which contains several art galleries is a famous site in *Central Postdam.* Never Gaten, a lakeside Park here is a place to relax after seeing all the art exhibits in Sanssouchi Park. Right on the lake itself is the Marvel Palace which has now been restored. Cecilienhof here is known for its 1945

Postdam Conference and pictures of Churchill, Stalin and Truman, who participated in the conference are on display inside it.

Munich or *Munchen*, as the Germans say, is a big city situated in the *Western part of Germany.* In one of the quiet areas of the city, when I was about to jump a traffic light, an elderly lady pulled me back. She seemed upset on my violating traffic rules. I apologized straightaway and her face broke into a smile.

Lake Constance called the "*Swabian Ocean*" was another place I visited in Germany. This giant bulge in the sinewy course of the *Rhine* offered water sports and relaxation for the holidaymakers. The lake's southern part belongs to *Switzerland* and *Austria.* The German side of *Lake Constance* has crowded tourist places like *Constance, Meersburg* and island of *Lindau.*

Some small and beautiful towns along the River Rhine like *Singen, Ohningen* and *Stein Am Rhein* also the famous Rhinefall, which I visited, can be reached within 40 minutes by going west along the river. The largest waterfall in Europe, which drops twenty-three meters and makes a tremendous noise as 600 cubic meters of water comes crashing down every second. Passing by meadows, castles and ancient villages, this river presents some fascinating scenes.

AUSTRIA

Anyone touring Europe cannot afford to miss *Vienna (Wien)*, a city with rich historical background and the capital of **Austria**. It is this very city, which gave waltz to the world (my favourite dance), great composers made this place their home including people like Straws, Brahms, Beethoven, Mozart and Schubert. People interested in art have great affinity for this place. A visit to some historical sites located in the old city is a must for any tourist. St. Stephen's Cathedral is in the heart of the city. Architectural riches welcome you at every corner of the city. City Hall, the Greek Revival style parliament (The Athena Statue in particular), National Theatre and the Baroque St. Charles Church are worth mentioning. Its gothic architectural pointed arches rise high above the city. Its interior walls and pillars are decorated with fine statues, and its stone pulpit is particularly striking. Musical tradition alongside coffee houses and wine taverns characterize the Viennese culture.

Insbruck, another tourist attraction of Austria is situated in the very heart of the *Austrian Alps*. Its major attractions are Alpine resorts with excellent skiing facilities. Two of Austria's most famous resorts – St. Anton and Kitzbuhel, are found here. You can also pick up Bavarian cuckoo clocks from here.

ITALY

Rome, the capital of *Italy* is a vast city, which beckons every tourist of *Europe*. Its historical centre is relatively small and most of its major sights are within walking distance of each other. The world's smallest city **"***The Vatican City***"**, the Vatican Museum, the Sistine Chapel and the magnificent St. Peter's Church are incomparable and the home of architectural and artistic masterpieces by Michelangelo and Bernini which leave you awestruck. The Colosseum, the venue of gladiatorial fights reminded me of our ancient rulers who wielded absolute power and nobody could say anything to them. While there, I also harboured a wish and threw a coin at the majestic Trevi Fountain. The victor Emmanuel Piazza Venezia under which lies the tomb of the unknown soldier, Circus Maximums, known for its chariot races, the ancient ruins at Roman Forum are part of the site-seeing trip around the city. While visiting these places, one has to stop time and again, for coffee and pate (Pastries). It is rightly called the place of churches and museums. Italy's President lives at the Palazzo del Quinrinale. The place and its garden's are open for the public. *Rome* is a congested city full of winding lanes, by-lanes and streets. One can get lost in **Rome** and once that happens it is very difficult to get back on to your road. Pizzas and Cappuccino Coffee are world famous. You can have them to your heart's content.

Leaning Tower of *Pisa* is a world-famous site in Italy which occupies a prime place on the tourist's map. One gets spell bound while approaching this precariously leaning Tower. But having seen it, shopping for souvenirs was more enjoyable. One could haggle with local women. Italians are more like us Indians, little loud and noisy. I picked up some beautiful scarves and marble figurines from there as souvenirs.

Venice is one of the most beautiful cities of *Europe*. I am sure seeing *Venice* is everyone's dream. Best way to see this beauty is by walking. Perhaps no other city in the world has inspired some of the greatest writers and travellers all through the ages as this unique city is built on 117 small islands with 150 canals and more than 400 bridges. One can reach St. Mark's Square by Gondola or a boat to the heart of the city of *Venice*. While sailing over the wonderful lagoon city, one can catch a glimpse of the serene waters and its canals. On reaching the destination one can admire St. Mark's Square with its basilica, the Doge's Palace, the Campanile, and the Bridge of Sighs.

The beautiful *murano* or Venetian glass is world famous. One must visit a glass factory to have a look at the demonstration of how glass is blown. Also there are a lot of show rooms along with the canals, which sell a variety of goods that are inimitable. I went berserk trying to pick and choose some gifts for my friends and myself.

While touring *Italy*, a visit to Florance, a cradle of Renaissance, former home of the Medicis is a must. The Duomo, the Campanile and the Baptistry with its gate to paradise, Pizza Della Signoria and open air Museum of Sculptures and Sante Croce where Michelangelo, Galileo and many famous personalities are buried, are some of the famous sights in this town. The famous Ponte Vecchio Bridge across the rive Arno and the Pizzale Michelangelo with its impressive statue of David can also be seen here.

A visit to *Italy* can never be complete without seeing *Milan*, a big industrial city and the fashion capital of Italy. Most of its sights seeing places are in the old town, which is at the center of the city. Duomo, a cathedral constructed by Gian Galeezo Visconti in 1386, is a marvel. Its structure with its marble façade shaped into Pinnacles, statues and pillars are certainly unique. Unfortunately when we entered Duomo, it was closed from inside. A weekly tour of graceful Gallerie Vittorio Emanuele to La Scale, Milan's famous Opera House, castello Sforzesco at the end of Via Dante, a museum that has sculptures including Michelangelo's Pieta Rondanini were a memorable experience. Como is a beautiful lake near *Milan* from where one can see lovely mountains of *Switzerland*. This place is a popular holiday resort.

ENGLAND

On one of my trips to *London*, after paying a lot of excess baggage due to lot of shopping done by me, I finally checked in at Heathrow airport and was still left with a heavy bag and a heavy handbag to carry it all the way to the aircraft. One has to walk a lot on these big international airports and especially *London* where there is big air traffic. To carry these two heavy bags and no help, I was stopping every now and then because of terrible pain in both of my hands. No porter and no coolie. I had tears in my eyes. How difficult it must be for the coolies at the railway stations in *India* who carry heavy load on their heads from platform to the railway compartment. Thank God now that we have carts at some of the big railway platforms. I promised myself not to shop so much and overload myself with so much baggage.

City of London, the capital of *Great Britain*, is one of the most important financial centres in the world and also the largest city of *Europe*. One of its peculiar geographical features is the tidal river Thames, which divides the city into northern and southern halves. The underground rail system, popularly called the tube, makes most of it easily accessible.

I was lucky enough to see this city four times, and my longest stay was when I joined the institute to undergo the beautician's course. Since I was in and out of this place, I could see it at great length. It is also a shopper's paradise. Like all the big cities of *Europe*, this place too has a number of places like the Big Ben, Tower Bridge, St. Paul's Cathedral,

Oxford Street which has (an endless chain of department stores), Piccadily Circus, Leicester Square, elegant shops of Regent and Bond Streets, St. James' Palace and West Minister Abbey, Parliament House, Madam Tussaud's Wax Museum, Kensington Garden and Hyde Park, Queen's Victoria Memorial which no visitor to London can afford to miss. The ceremonial change of guards outside the Buckingham Palace attracts large crowds. London's famous shopping stores like Harrods in knight's Bridge, Selfridges on the Oxford street, Marks and Spencer, C&A and Tower Records, the best music shop in London are world famous. Bloomsbury is still synonymous with literary publishing worlds.

Windsor Palace, which is not too far from the heart of *London*, is of great historical value. Harrods had always been my favourite store. I made sure to visit it whenever I happened to be in *London*. I picked up some of the finest curios from there along with gifts for my family, which were always appreciated for its quality.

Queen Mary 2 (Cruise), sailing across Mediterranean

I had one of my most privileged trips on Queen Mary 2, the largest, longest, tallest, widest and grandest ocean liner ever built. It is a grand floating palace. On boarding it, one could have a royal trip. Queen Mary 2 is a legend on the seas, a queen among queens, known for the high style, which has attracted celebrities and actors. An authentic ocean liner it has the strength to cut through the mighty *Atlantic* and the power to sustain high speed while providing comfortable and stable journey for the guests .

Queen Mary has six storeys and a vast atrium

from which you can see some remarkable sites on every turn. Its wide spacious hallways and broad teak Deck are worth seeing. Queen Room, noted for the largest dance floor at sea, exquisite dining hall, luxurious cabins, veuve clicquot champagne Bar are some of its unique features. A Hermes boutique and her Cunard Royal Spa rival the very best in the world. It is certainly a magnificent resort on the planet representing English culture. The staff looking after the guests is remarkably caring and efficient. Nowhere in the world one is pampered to this extent. It happened to be one of my most relaxing holidays.

GREECE

Since *Athens* in *Greece* has a history of Greek religion, culture and mythology, I took this opportunity sailing on Queen Mary 2 to visit *Athens.* Delphi, a home and the sanctuary of the oracle of the Greek God Apollo was believed to be the "Naval of the world" by ancient Greeks. It was the largest religious and spiritual center in Hellas. People from all over the world came to listen to the priestess's prophecy. The fame of this place had spread throughout the *Mediterranean.* Sanctuary's renown remained undimmed until Christianity came to prevail and idolatry was banned because of which this sanctuary was abandoned.

Besides the museums, Acropolis and old monuments, I enjoyed going to the beautiful islands like *Poros, Hydra* and *Aegina. Poros*, the smallest of the three islands is a lush green island, covered with lemon and pine trees. It has small and narrow streets where one can pick up hand embroidered linen and gift items. *Aegina* which is the largest island is famous for its pistachio groves which sustain its economy. Pistachio when fresh, has a magnificent colour. I had never seen such large fresh and sweet pastachio ever before. This place has a very rich past and a fascinating present. In *Hydra* one can admire the unique architecture of its houses, its crystal clear beaches and famous jewellery and boutique shops. This island attracts a large number of painters and photographers.

The site of ancient *Olypia* is just half a km. away from the modern town of Athens, surrounded by the green foothills of Mt. Kronion. The first Olympics was staged here in 776 BC. The sprawling runs of the temple of Zeus to whom the games were dedicated are the dominating feature of this place.

Besides *Olypia*, being sports person myself, I specially visited *Munich*, a train journey took me to the Great Olympic village; *Barcelona* in *Spain* where 1992 Olympics took place; *Atlanta* in the *USA* where Olympics were held in 1996 and *Athens* in *Greece*, which hosted Olympics in 2004.

SPAIN

I visited *Barcelona* in *Spain* in the month of August 2000 by taking a flight from *Geneva*. It was a very thrilling experience. In doing so, I was also guided by the tourist office at *Geneva* that informed me about the tourist buses (The red line and the blue line) which made my trip so easy. I had not travelled this way in any other country. *Barcelona* is a big city and places of interest and sight seeing are many. The only thing one had to do was to collect a guide map from a tourist office and then choose your destination. My first desire was to see great Antonio Gaudi's creations which had made him famous all over the world. His most emblematic work, the Sagrade Familia had become a symbol of

Barcelona all over the world. Gaudi took up this work in 1883, with a desire to make it a cathedral for the twentieth century with a view to explain the mysteries of faith through his architecture. He died in 1926. Ever since the building work has progressed erratically. The Avinguda Gaudi, a pedestrian boulevard, runs from the Sagrada Familia as far as Domenech 1 Montaner's Modernist Hospital de la Sanata Creu 1 de Sant Pau. The Casa Mila (La Pedrera) by Gaudi is considered the pinnacle of the modernist movement with its impressive undulating stone façade. His work in designing the attic and the rooftop Drawings, Photographs and Audiovisual displays give us an insight into the work of Gaudi (1852-1926).

Pedralbes Monastery, Poble Espanyol Placa Espanya where most of the buildings around are on Montijuic, the adjacent hill. The fountain designed by Jijola, a disciple of Gaudi, Venetiion towers, Museu National d' art de Catalunya. Allena Olimpica, MNAC, Port Vell (The liveliest and a relaxing area in *Barcelona*) Maremagnum a complex built over the sea for shopping, and savouring seafood and watching latest fashion, Vila Olimpica (olimpic village) Barri Gotic (city's medieval buildings) Pelai – Centres d' Artcontemporari and a famous football club of *Barcelona* are some of the famous sites in this area.

PALACES

The Palaces have especially fascinated me because I come from *Rajasthan*, a state known for its palaces and historical monuments. Palaces have always been at the top of the list of places that I wanted to see. Other sites were given a secondary place. Palaces give me a chance to learn the history of that era. Schonbrun Palace in *Vienna* (*Austria*), which I saw, has extensive gardens enlivened by several fountains. Its interior crystal chandeliers and gilded ornaments with frescoed ceilings give it a majestic look. One can have a lovely view of the Schonbrun Palace from the Gloriett Monument located on a hill right behind the Palace.

Another palace of *Vienna*, Belvedere Palace, has the famous Austrian Art Gallery located inside, which occupies two main buildings. Some interesting baroque pieces are on display, but the upper part of Belvedere Palace exhibits the works of Egon Schiele, Gustau Klimt and other famous Austrian artists from 19th and 20th centuries. The palace has spacious gardens around it and one can have a good view of the city from it.

Schloss Sanssouci Palace in *Berlin*, located in Sanssouci Park, has some of the most majestically decorated interiors. The vast stretches of greenery around the palace give it a royal look and remind you of the olden days of Kings and Queens.

Palau Reial Palace in *Barcelona* (*Spain*) too depicts the rich Spanish art and culture. The Ceramics Museum there displays a vast collection of glazed ceramic pieces made in *Spain* from the 11th century to the present day.

Royal Palace in *Amsterdam* is the home of Dutch royalty, but it remains unoccupied most of the time as they prefer their residence in *Hague*.

Buckingham Palace in *London* has been the seat of the greatest empire the world has ever known. The staterooms which are open to the public, situated in the west-wing of Buckingham Palace are very well maintained. How rich are its interiors?

One has to see to believe how richly its Green Drawing room, Throne Room, Silk Tapestry Room, Blue Drawing Room, White Drawing Room, State Dining Room, Picture Gallery, East Gallery, Gross Gallery and West Gallery are decorated. The outside of the palace does not give the appearance of richness as its interiors.

The Royal Imperial palace in *Tokyo* (*Japan*) is the official residence of the Japanese Emperor and the imperial family. It is not open to public. Its architectural design has been executed in typical Japanese style and the gardens around it are the specimens of exquisite beauty.

Kings Palace in *Kuala Lumpur* (*Malaysia*) is quite different from the above Palaces because it is built according to the well-developed designs of Islamic architecture.

THE MUSEUMS (EUROPE)

The Museum *Picasso* in *Barcelona* (*Spain*) has the world's largest and almost complete collection of the young Picasso's works. The works extending from the period 1890 to 1997, show various stages in the development of his creative endeavour ultimately making him the master of his craft. I almost ran amok buying the prints of those beautiful oil paintings.

Though *Paris* (*France*) has more than 100 museums, Lourve is by far the most popular and the most famous museum. Leonardo de Vince's Mona Lisa occupies a pride of place over there. This museum requires several serious visits to have the briefest glimpse of the masterpieces of art to be found in it amongst which The Winged Victory of Samothrace and Venice de Milo are the ones not to be missed.

The Catalan History Museum in *Barcelona* (*Spain*) offers a journey through the history of Catalonia from prehistoric to the present day.

The Rijksmuseum in *Amsterdam* has Netherland's largest art collection. It displays the works of artists from the 15th and the 19th centuries and has Rambrandt's famous Night Watch. One has to pay several visits, like to Lourve in Paris, to see it fully.

National Archeological Museum of *Athens* in *Greece* is a crowd puller and is the topmost museum in the country where one finds relics from all the major archaeological sites including the magnificent, exquisitely carved, gold arte-facts from Mycenac and the spectacular Minoan fresco from Santorini (Thira). Benaki Museum there named after Antoine Benaki Collection is also worth seeing. The collection includes specimens of ancient Persian and Byzantine and Chinese collection of ceramics, Icons and two El Greco paintings and some classic costumes.

The Acropolis (museum) in *Athens* shows the true picture of this place as it was in its heyday. The ruins show how magnificent and powerful these countries must have been.

The museum at Delphi in *Athens* too points to the glorious history of the Greek people. One can guess fro the ruins in this place how rich the Greek civilization must have been at that point of time.

Geneva in *Switzerland* has more than thirty museums. The Natural History Museum is somewhat different from other museums and has a unique collection of taxidermic beautiful birds, fishes, lions, elephants and tigers. It was a treat watching small children getting excited seeing them.

The British Museum in *London* has the greatest collection of antiquities and one has to have lot of time to see all of it. The pains the British Government has taken in restoring and preserving their heritage is amazing. The Museum of *London* depicts the history of *London* from the time of Romans to this day.

SQUARES (EUROPE)

San Marco square in *Venice (Italy)* is one of the most famous squares in the world. San Marco was described by Napoleon as the finest drawing room in *Europe*. The *Piazza* hosts flocks of pigeons and tourists both competing for space in the high season. I can never forget this place. Initially in early eighties, I was to come here on a tour from *Munich*. I had an O.K. ticket but forgot about it on that particular day. That's why I missed the group of friends I was supposed to join at San Marco (St. Marks) Square. Later when I saw the jam packed crowd there I realized I could not have possibly found my friends in Venice's most famous place. It was a blessing in disguise as the next day, I joined them at another station. I get goose pimples whenever I think of myself being left all alone at St. Marks Square, an experience that I had on my second trip. Booking at any hotel was impossible without advance notice. In case I would not have found my friends, I'd have been in deep trouble.

St. Peter's Basilica and Square in *Rome (Italy)* is one of the most famous churches in the Christian world as St. Peter was buried here. This square is considered a masterpiece of artistic endeavour.

Duomo square in *Milan (Italy)* – Sight seeing areas and the shopping streets starts from here. Even the metro station is next door.

Place de Vosges in *Paris (France)* is famous for its up markets, art galleries, antique shops and saloons. It is an attractive place and is always crowded by tourists and shoppers.

Place de Catalunya in *Barcelone (Spain)* – this square is the starting point of the city's main streets and avenues such as La Rambla, a world famous boulevard renowned for its jostling crowds and the Placa Espanya.

Dam Square in *Amsterdam (Netherlands)* is the best place to start seeing the city. This is the spot where the Amstel River was dammed in the 13th century, giving the city its name. It is the intersection where the surging crowds from the incoming pedestrians and shopping streets intermingle.

Trafalgar Square in *London* raised to commemorate Britain's naval victory over Napoleonic *France* is very famous and most talked of. In fact, Trafalgar Square as well as Leicester Square are two landmarks which no tourist can afford to miss.

JAPAN

In the year 1992, I visited *Japan.* Its culture, politeness and modesty of its people impressed me the most. One of the most prominent characteristic of Japanese people is their tremendous sense of duty & discipline. The language was bit difficult to understand but people being so helpful, I could make my way through. An average person there reads a lot. No wonder the young generation has so many persons wearing reading glasses. It is a nation where women play a prominent role. Their culture makes them lady-like, both at home as well as at the work place. It is a pleasure watching them at big shopping malls where they stand on either side of escalators and as the customers go up and down, they willingly bow their heads before their customers as a mark of courtesy, while dressed up in their elegant silk kimonos. They truly deserved to be called ladies. There is an old saying, "If you have a British Passport, American dollars and a Japanese wife, you don't need anything else in the world." How true!

Tokyo is certainly one of the most expensive cities in the world. Tokyo Tower is very fascinating from top of it you can see the whole city. Huge flyovers in *Tokyo* are the marvels of engineering.

Hiroshima - The immense progress made by this city after what it went through during the World War II is simply amazing. The credit for it goes to every Japanese citizen. It was sad to see *Hiroshima's* Peace Memorial Museum depicting one of the worst tragedies of humanity. One can only imagine the plight of people after atomic bomb was dropped on *Hiroshima* and *Nagasaki*. Japanese people are basically creative and hard working. Give them a dirty place or a drain, they would create a beautiful garden or a beautiful spot out of it. The art of Ikebana flower arrangement is their creation and a gift to the world. It seems every citizen had taken a vow after the World War II to make this country a better nation than what it was ever before. "Flame of Peace" is one of the memorials lit in August, 1964. The flame will now be extinguished only when nuclear weapons disappear from the world. I can never forget the enjoyable experience of having a ride on the then fastest train in the world, "*Shenkanzen*" from **Tokyo** to *Hiroshima* and back.

Sitting around a small dining table bare feet and enjoying the Japanese delicacies like fish, soups cooked with vegetables & meats and boiled rice is a pleasant experience. These things are literally cooked by every individual on the dining table itself which is something unique. Sitting down and eating was not a problem for me because in most of our homes people still sit together on the floor and eat on ceremonial occasions in a group of four.

SOUTH EAST ASIA

I found *Singapore*, the cleanest and most orderly city. The airport itself is beautiful, immaculately clean and beautified with waterfalls. Shopping at the famous malls at Orchard Road or Mustafa Market is a pleasure. It is a small place but very well organized. Interesting places like China Town, City Hall, Parliament House and little India are worth seeing. Seeing Jurong Bird Park, a home to 7000 birds of 600 species displayed in a huge enclosure was a sheer pleasure. A 98 ft waterfall in the aviary is the world's highest man-made waterfall. Orchid Park, which has a vast collection of different coloured orchids is spectacular. At this park, one can select orchid-designed jewellery in small shops. Things like pendants, earrings and broaches are unique and have a charm of their own.

Sentosa Island, which houses a huge park, is the national symbol of *Singapore*. The Merilion Sentosa Island is the largest and the best-known offshore island of *Singapore*. It is also the one, which is closest to the main land and has many attractions. I saw the first musical fountain show here for the first time in my life. The sound, light and laser extravaganza charmed the whole crowd.

Bangkok, the capital of *Thailand* has lately become famous for green and red Thai curries cooked with chicken cubes or fish. The city has some of the most beautiful local restaurants where the food is served by beautiful Thai women, dressed up in their traditional costumes. They are soft spoken and have lovely manners and to be treated by them in the right royal manner is itself an experience. The food is delicious!

Whenever I visited *Bangkok*, I had a long list of shopping. One can shop there in departmental stores and shopping malls to one's heart content. The cotton stuff sold there is beautiful and comparatively cheaper than in other countries.

Beautiful temples, especially *Wat Traimit* and *Wat Pho* are great tourist attractions. The statue of Buddha at *Wat Traimit* is made from solid gold weighing 5.5 tons. *Wat Pho* has the statue of reclining Buddha which is the largest and oldest in *Bangkok*. The famous Wat Benchamabophot Monastry was built with white Italian Marble from Carrara in accordance with Thai temple architecture. The big modern buildings there are impressive and the hospitality of 5 star hotels is memorable. Bangkok has a flourishing orchids business. The flowers are beautifully packed with glass tubes containing water for the stems which keep the flowers fresh for days together.

I also enjoyed visiting *Pattaya*, a Thai village, famous for its beach retreat. The place is enlivened with cultural shows, comprising traditional dance and music and Thai martial arts. The local dances in the traditional costumes with their typical slow movements and rhythm are very graceful. This place is famous for its massage parlours. Thai women are the best masseurs. Tourists often indulge in it for relaxation.

Coral Island: To have a joy ride in glass-bottomed boat is a must. To see the world of colorful corals and beautiful underwater life is an amazing experience. The water sports like wind surfing, snorkeling and parasailing provide another outlet for fun-loving people.

Watching *Alcazar* night show, with over 100 professionals dancing in dazzling costumes was a lifetime experience. I was told some of the men who participate in it have undergone an operation to change their sex.

Kuala Lumpur (Malaysia): In 1986, when I visited *Kuala Lumpur*, I wore a *burkha* (a *muslim* veil) for the first time, while entering the national Mosque. No woman was allowed to get in without covering herself from head to foot. So I hired *burkha* after which I was allowed to see this air-conditioned mosque with beautiful carpets spread for those who went in to pray. It was worthwhile to see such a mosque made in accordance with Islamic architecture. Local *muslim* women keep their hair covered with scarves and are also soft spoken. The other interesting places I saw there were the King's Palace, commercial centre and the National monument. It is a very green city with beautiful green plants growing everywhere.

Genting Highlands situated 2000 meters above the sea level is also a great tourist attraction of *Malaysia*. A cable car ride took us up to *Genting* city. The cable ride was nice and slow. There was breath-taking scenery all along the way with cool mountain air. This city offers all sorts of entertainment. It was difficult for me to try everything in half a day, but I availed of whatever opportunities came my way in that short span of time.

Penang is a small town in *Malaysia*. When I landed there, I thought it looked like *Kerala*, green with thick forests. People were simple and hospitable. From here we went by a coach crossing a huge bridge. What an invention! Bamboo handicrafts, made of bamboo strips are speciality of this place.

UNITED STATES OF AMERICA

U.S.A. is a great country and its people are friendly and full of life and humour. It is a freedom loving nation. People work hard and also enjoy life. They get whatever they want. Every state has weekend recreation places where people enjoy all sorts of entertainment facilities. Particularly, children and youth are truly pampered. On one of my trips to ***Michigan*** in 1995, I saw people jogging at any time of the day and wishing each other, "Have a nice day". In response to which everyone said, "You too". These little gestures would put an outsider at ease. *Michigan State* is one of the 49 states of *U.S.A.* It is named after the *Michigan lake*, the largest lake in the world. *Mickinac* island Surrey is located on this lake. Fort Michil Mackinee, which is famous for American war of Independence, too is located here. ***Mt. Pleasant***, a small town in *Michigan*, is a pleasant town. I stayed there for quite some time during my many visits to *Michigan*. The jogging tracks along the parks and roadside are good. Once while jogging, I got tired and sat under an apple tree. A fully ripe red apple fell on me. Suddenly I looked up and found the tree was full of red apples.

I wiped it with my hands and began to munch it. A young girl who too was jogging saw me having the apple. She too stopped there and plucked an apple. As she took the first bite, she looked at me and said, "Isn't it delicious? I never noticed the apple tree before!" We both giggled and I said, "You have it so good over here, had this apple tree been in our country, not a single apple would have been left by now." Later I started noticing a few pear and apple trees along the roads and on some patches of grassy areas.

New York: The Statue of Liberty standing on sprawling 12 acres' estuary in the harbour can be seen from miles together. Whether you are in a ship or an aircraft, you know you are in *New York*. The John F. Kennedy Airport's airstrip is right on the edge of the ocean. And while landing one feels as though the aircraft is going to land on the water.

Manhattan is a very much talked about place in *USA* and if you have a house or an office there you are considered a rich guy. Central Park in the heart of *Manhattan* is one of the city's main attractions. Le Ciroue N.Y. Palace Hotel there is a renowned oranate French restaurant and a watering hole of highflying socialites and celebrities. Peter Luger, steak house in Brooklyn is worth a trip to that place. The 21 club has a long history of gourmet food. The famous Rockfeller Center has St. Patricks Cathedral, Radio City, Music Hall, The NBC studios and The Rainbow Room in its vicinity.

Los Angeles is a city known for its glamour all over the world. It has many sights of interest like any big city. *Hollywood* being here, people flock to see the famous Universal Studio. Here you do not watch the films, but see the famous sets from various films, thrilling stunts, artificially created floods, earthquakes and sharks as you saw in the movie "Jaw". Along the way just as in the Tramp, a famous movie, tempt fate as you venture inside the acurssed mummy's tomb, where skeleton of warriors wait for fresh human victims, and immerse yourself in movie magic at the new special effects studios. You also have different shows of all the famous movies like Spiderman Rocks, Blast Zone, Shrekbact To The Future, etc.

Beverley Hills and famous Disneyland are two places that no one should miss. Right from my childhood days, it was my dream to stay for a couple of days at **Disneyland**, as one needs a lot of time to spend in this wondrous land. **Santa Monica** and **Malibu**, small places near ***L.A.*** are worth visiting. ***Chicago*** *(Illinois)* and ***Columbus*** *(Ohio)* too are among some great cities of the world. ***Miami*** *(Florida)*, a place famous for its beaches and a popular resort for the ***Hollywood*** stars that go there to relax. *Miami* has hosted some of the most wonderful fashion shows and Miss World and *Miss Universe* competitions. ***Florida*** is also famous for its renowned golf courses at *Palm Beach* and *Pebble Beach* and of course a home during the winters for many North Americans who want to be away from the freezing cold. ***Orlando***, a modern *Disneyland* is spread in a vast area and one needs time to see it from one end to the other.

Atlanta has rich history and a peculiar charm of its own. The city offers a true glimpse of southern *America. Painting* in the Round is one of the most popular touring centres of *Atlanta.* It is a mammoth creation which is 42 feet high and 358 feet in circumference, depicting the battle of *Atlanta.* Viewing the battle scope (created in 1886) from theater-style seats on a rotating platform is a unique experience. Section of the poignant scene is spotlighted as its narration and vivid sound effects recreate that searing July-Aug in 1864. Also on show is the **Texas**, the railroad engine that pursued the General in the Andrew Raid. Stone Mountain with face is the world's largest granite monolith, rising 825 feet above a 3200 area. Te lake-studded park, which has the paddle-wheel riverboat, scarlet O'Hara, a scenic railroad, an antebellum plantation, a natural - habitat zoo are worth seeing. Featured on the mountain's northern face is the world's largest carving, featuring the faces of confederate President Jefferson, Davis, General Robert E. Lee and General Stonewall Jackson. The Chattahoochee River there is national recreation area for those who want to indulge in rafting and canoeing.

NEPAL

Kathmandu valley, the capital city of *Nepal*, which I visited a number of times, is the home of the ancient and sophisticated *Newari* culture. They are the creators of the splendid civilization of three cities - *Kathmandu, Patan* and *Bhaktapur*. The skillfully built temples and palaces embellished with delicately engraved stones, metal images and carved wooden columns and pillars are marvellous architectural creations.

Rohit had a huge house, beautifully located on a hilltop over looking the valley of *Kathmandu*. The view was soothing to the eyes...

There are many beautiful temples but *Pashupatinath* and *Budhanikanatha* temples are the most famous. The temple of Lord Shiva - *Pashupatinath* has a special place in my heart. One incident always makes me think and pray because of an experience which I had over there. Nepal has a very big following of Sai Baba of *Puttaparthi* and *Shirdhi Sai Baba.* It is amazing to see big pictures of both of them in the leading department stores, shops and in peoples' homes. The temple of Sai Baba (Puttaparthi) which I saw in *Kathmandu* is one of the nicest. Since I was seeing so many of Baba's pictures every where, I became curious to find out if there was a centre which I could visit on Thursdays to attend the programme for the recitation of devotional songs. To my surprise I suddenly saw a white coloured van with painted pictures of Sai Baba on both sides and the name of the centre and the telephone number written down on it, coming out of the main gate of Pashupatinath temple! I collected my bag and shoes from outside, as you're not supposed to take anything made of leather inside the temple. I pulled out my diary and jotted down the telephone number. The volunteer who was driving the van came back. I was surprised even more to see the van being allowed to come right up to the main gate of the temple. The parking was quite far off from the temple. The volunteer not only explained to me where the centre was but also took me in the same van to the centre. My car followed the van. That's how I could attend Thursday's programmes. Pashupatinath is one of the holiest shrines for Hindus. No one except Hindus is allowed to go in. Visitors can clearly see its two tiered golden roof and silver door from outside. Another famous temple Budhanilkanatha has the statue of Lord Vishnu, reclining, on a bed of snakes. This is one of the masterpieces of stone sculptures of the Lichchavi period. Swayambhunath, one of the most glorious Buddhist *Chaityas,* is situated on a hill top and gives a beautiful view of the *Kathmandu* valley.

Bhaktapur city lies about 14 km. east of the *Kathmandu.* It is renowned for its elegant carved art, fabulous culture, colourful festivals, traditional dances performed in typical *Newari* style. The ancient city of *Patan* lying 5 km. South East of *Kathmandu. Patan Durbar* Square is full of ancient Palaces, temples and shrines with exquisite carvings.

Gokarna – A famous forest Golf Resort on the North Eastern side of eastern *Kathmandu* city is spread out in 470 acres in the ancient *Gokarna* forest with the majestic *Himalayas*, better known as the rooftop of the world, providing a dramatic backdrop.

Pokhara valley is famous for sight seeing. One either flies or goes by road to this valley from *Kathmandu.* It is famous for Davis Fall which has 150 ft fall into the lake water which disappears into a big hole. *Sarangkot* or *Naudanda* are famous for the sunrise tour in the central part of the *Pokhara* valley. Mount *Fishtail* and *Annapurna* ranges covered with snow, to the north have bird's eye view of *Pokhara* town and lake *Phewa* to the southeast along with lake Begnes and Rupa. Trekking and mountaineering is best way to experience Nepal's natural beauty.

Chitwan is one of the finest national parks of *Asia* renowned for its dense jungles and profusion of wild life. It has top class tourist lodges. *Chitwan* means the heart of the jungle. Wildlife comprises the rare one-horned rhinoceros, several species of deer, sloth bear, leopard, wild boar. It also has fresh water dolphins, crocodiles and Royal Bengal Tigers. One can enjoy excursion on elephant's back, canoe trips along the jungle track. Our whole family went together, had an experience of a lifetime. Cars were parked 1 km outside the park and we had to go on elephant's back in the jungles.

PAKISTAN

Pakistan - I visited *Pakistan* four times during 1989 to 2005. During my various visits I stayed in *Karachi, Hyderabad (Sindh), Umerkot, Islamabad, Rawalpindi, Murree* and *Lahore.*

Pakistan has small aristocracy, some middle class and a large number of people who may be classified as poor. I met erstwhile politicians, Jagirdars and the common people in the places I visited. ***Karachi*** was one place where I stayed for longer duration. The women there are beautiful and very well dressed! Their culture speaks volumes of the background they come from. *Karachi,* being coastal city, is climatically more like *Bombay.* It has beautiful beaches, especially lit up at night with flooded lights, lovely shopping malls, nice restaurants and is a good place to live especially during winters. *Quaid-E-Azam's Mazar* here is an object of reverence for all Pakistanis. *Sindh* club too is still very famous. *Agha Khan Hospital* with its splendid Spa and health club is worth a visit.

The hospitality and large heartedness of *Pakistani* people cannot be compared with any other place. Once you go to anyone's house as a guest, you are given the royal treatment and Pakistani delicacies are spread out before you. You cannot taste even half the spread. People are generally polite. You notice even in the market place that the shopkeepers are very polite. They respect their women in public places too. A woman is safe when out of home.

The Non-vegetarian dishes in Pakistan are

delicious and Pakistanis are especially fond of non-vegetarian food. It is a treat to visit Pakistan during *Ramzan* which is the best time to taste a variety of special dishes.

Islamabad, the capital of *Pakistan* is a modern and one of the most beautiful cities. It has nice residential, public buildings and a flourishing market place. Being close to *Murree*, which is a hill station, the climate is cool. Like *Singapore*, it is a well organised place. *Faisal Masjid* is very famous spot of *Islamabad* and late President *Zia-Ul Haq* was given the highest respect by the Pakistani people for burying him next to the Masjid.

Rawalpindi is a small town close to *Islamabad*. Having a large population, it is very congested. Wherever you go, you come across large crowds. One sees lots of Afghans going around selling beautifully-woven carpets. It is pleasure seeing them persuading people to sell their stuff, by reducing the prices for those who can bargain with them. They are an innocent looking people and their children are especially good looking. "*The Barda Market*" is famous for selling all sorts of things from South East Asia.

Lahore, the capital of Pakistani *Punjab* is a historic city inhabited by affluent people. It is a place of industrialists, businessmen, shopkeepers and restaurant owners and is the hub of the fashion designers. It's a very green city.

